1977

I Never Sang
for My Father

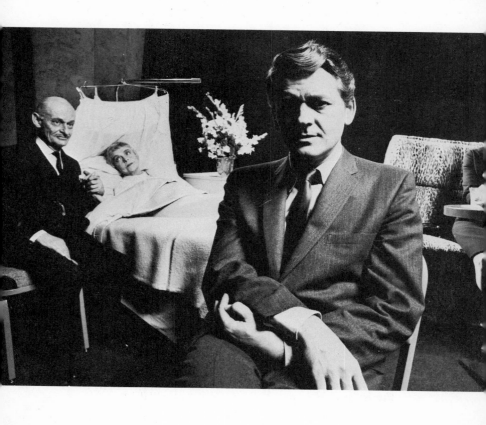

I Never Sang

for My Father

ROBERT ANDERSON

Random House New York

Photographs by courtesy of Martha Swope and Henri Dauman

Library of Congress Catalogue Card Number: 68–19594

Manufactured in the United States of America

for
ALAN SCHNEIDER
and
GILBERT CATES

I NEVER SANG FOR MY FATHER *was first presented on January 25, 1968, by Gilbert Gates in association with Doris Vidor at the Longacre Theatre, New York City, with the following cast:*

(In order of appearance)

GENE GARRISON	Hal Holbrook
PORTER	Earl Sydnor
TOM GARRISON	Alan Webb
MARGARET GARRISON	Lillian Gish
MARY	Sloane Shelton
NURSE	Laurinda Barrett
REVEREND PELL	Allan Frank
MARVIN SCOTT	Matt Crowley
WAITER	James A. Spearman
DR. MAYBERRY	Daniel Keyes
ALICE	Teresa Wright

Directed by Alan Schneider
Scenery and Lighting by Jo Mielziner
Costumes by Theoni V. Aldredge

SYNOPSIS OF SCENES

The time is the present and the past.
The places are New York City and a town in
Westchester County.

Act One

There are no sets. Lighting is the chief means for setting the stage.

A man comes from the shadows in the rear. He is GENE GARRISON, *age forty. He checks his watch. A* PORTER *passes through with a baggage cart.*

GENE   I wonder if you could help me. (*The* PORTER *stops*) My father and mother are coming in on the Seaboard Express from Florida. I'd like a wheelchair for my mother if I could get one.

PORTER   You have the car number?

GENE   Yes. (*He checks a slip of paper*) One-oh-seven.

PORTER   Due in at three ten. I'll meet you on the platform.

GENE   Thank you. (*The* PORTER *moves away and off.* GENE *comes down and addresses the audience*) Death ends a life, but it does not end a relationship, which struggles on in the survivor's mind toward some final resolution, some clear meaning, which it perhaps never finds. (*He changes the mood*) Pennsylvania Station, New York, a few years ago. My mother and father were returning from Florida. They were both bored in Florida, but they had been going each winter for a number of years. If they didn't go, my father came down with pneumonia and my mother's joints stiffened cruelly with arthritis. My mother read a

3

great deal, liked to play bridge and chatter and laugh gaily with "the girls" . . . make her eyes sparkle in a way she had and pretend that she had not had two operations for cancer, three heart attacks and painful arthritis . . . She used to say, "Old age takes courage." She had it. My father, though he had never been in the service, had the air of a retired brigadier general. He read the newspapers, all editions, presumably to help him make decisions about his investments. He watched Westerns on television and told anyone who would listen the story of his life. I loved my mother . . . I wanted to love my father . . .

> (*The lights come up on another area of the stage, where the* PORTER *is already standing with the wheelchair and baggage cart.* TOM GARRISON *is standing amid the suitcases which have been piled up on the platform. He is a handsome man, almost eighty, erect in his bearing, neat in his dress. He speaks distinctly, and when he is irritated, his voice takes on a hard, harsh edge. At the moment he is irritated, slightly bewildered, on the brink of exasperation*)

TOM   We had four bags. I don't see any of them. We had one in the compartment with us. That can't have been lost.

> (*He fumes for a moment. As* GENE *watches his father for a moment, we can see in his face something of his feelings of tension. On the surface he shows great kindness and consideration for the old man. Underneath there is usually considerable strain*)

GENE   Hello, Dad.

4

TOM (*Beaming*)   Well, Gene, as I live and breathe. This *is* a surprise.

GENE   I wrote you I'd be here.

TOM   Did you? Well, my mind is like a sieve. (*They have shaken hands and kissed each other on the cheek*) Am I glad to see you! They've lost all our bags.

GENE   I'm sure they're somewhere, Dad.

TOM (*Firmly*)   No. I've looked. It's damnable!

GENE   Well, let's just take it easy. I'll handle it.
(*He looks around at the luggage piled on the platform*)

TOM   I'm confident we had four bags.

GENE (*Quietly showing the redcap*)   There's one . . . They'll show up. Where's mother?

TOM   What? . . . Oh, she's still on the train. Wait a minute. Are you sure that's ours?
(*He looks around for bags, fussing and fuming. He shakes his head in exasperation with the world*)

GENE   Yes, Dad. You just relax now.
(TOM *is seized with a fit of coughing*)

TOM (*Is exasperated at the cough*)   Damn cough. You know the wind never stops blowing down there.

GENE   Don't worry about anything now, Dad. We've got a porter, and everything's under control. (TOM *snorts at this idea. The redcap proceeds in a quiet, efficient and amused way to work the luggage*) I brought a wheelchair for Mother.

TOM   Oh. That's very considerate of you.

GENE   I'll go get her.

TOM   I didn't hear you.

GENE (*Raising his voice*)   I said I'll go get Mother.

TOM   Yes, you do that. I've got to get these damned bags straightened out.
        (*His rage and confusion are rising*)

GENE (*To the* PORTER)   There's one. The gray one.

TOM   That's not ours.

GENE (*Patient but irritated*)   Yes, it is, Dad.

TOM   No. Now wait. We don't want to get the wrong bags. Mine is brown.

GENE   The old one was brown, Dad. I got you a new one this year for the trip.

TOM (*Smiling reasonably*)   Now. Gene. I've had the bag in Florida all winter. I should know.

6

GENE   Dad. Please . . . Please let me handle this.

TOM (*Barks out an order to his son without looking at him*)
You go get your mother. I'll take care of the bags.
(GENE's *mouth thins to a line of annoyance. He
points out another bag to the* PORTER, *who is amused.*
GENE *moves with the wheelchair to another area of
the stage, where his mother,* MARGARET GARRISON, *is
sitting.* MARGARET *is waiting patiently. She is sev-
enty-eight, still a pretty woman. She has great spirit
and a smile that lights up her whole face. She is a
good sport about her problems. When she is put out,
she says "darn" and not "damn." She is devoted to
her son, but she is not the possessive and smothering
mother. She is wearing a white orchid on her mink
stole*)

GENE   Hello, Mother.

MARGARET (*Her face lights up*)   Well, Gene. (*She opens
her arms, but remains seated. They embrace*) Oh, my, it's
good to see you.
(*This with real feeling as she holds her son close to
her*)

GENE (*When he draws away*)   You look wonderful.

MARGARET   What?

GENE (*Raises his voice slightly. His mother wears a hearing
aid*)   You look wonderful.

7

MARGARET (*Little-girl coy*) Oh . . . a little rouge . . . This is your Easter orchid. I had them keep it in the icebox in the hotel. This is the fourth time I've worn it.

GENE You sure get mileage out of those things.

MARGARET (*Raising her voice slightly*) I say it's the fourth time I've worn it . . . Some of the other ladies had orchids for Easter, but mine was the only white one. (*She knows she is being snobbishly proud and smiles as she pokes at the bow*) I was hoping it would last so you could see it.

GENE How do you feel?

MARGARET (*Serious, pouting*) I'm all right, but your father . . . did you see him out there?

GENE Yes.

MARGARET He's sick and he won't do anything about it.

GENE I heard his cough.

MARGARET It makes me so darned mad. I couldn't get him to see a doctor.

GENE Why not?

MARGARET Oh, he's afraid they'd send him a big bill. He says he'll see Mayberry tomorrow . . . But I can't tell you

8

what it's been like. You tell him. Tell him he's got to see a doctor. He's got me sick with worry.

(*She starts to cry*)

GENE (*Comforts her*) I'll get him to a doctor, Mother. Don't you worry.

MARGARET He makes me so mad. He coughs all night and keeps us both awake. Poor man, he's skin and bone . . . And he's getting so forgetful. This morning he woke up here on the train and he asked me where we were going.

GENE Well, Mother, he's almost eighty.

MARGARET Oh, I know. And he's a remarkable man. Stands so straight. Everyone down there always comments on how handsome your father is . . . But I've given up. You get him to a doctor.

GENE I've got a wheelchair for you, Mother. Save you the long walk up the ramp.

MARGARET Oh, my precious. What would we ever do without you?

GENE (*He is always embarrassed by these expressions of love and gratitude*) Oh, you manage pretty well.

(*He helps her up from the chair, and she gives him a big hug as she stands . . . and looks at him*)

MARGARET Oh, you're a sight for sore eyes.

GENE (*Embarrassed by the intensity*) It's good to see you.

MARGARET (*She sits in the wheelchair*) You know, much as we appreciate your coming to meet us . . . I say, much as we appreciate your coming like this, the last thing in the world I'd want to do is take you away from your work.

GENE You're not, Mother.
  (*Father coughs his hacking cough*)

MARGARET Do you hear that? I'm so worried and so darned mad.
  (*They arrive at the platform area*)

TOM Oh, Gene, this is damnable. They've lost a suitcase. We had four suitcases.

GENE Let's see, Dad. There are four there.

TOM Where?

GENE Under the others. See?

TOM That's not ours.

GENE Yes. Your new one.

TOM Well, I'm certainly glad you're here. My mind's like a sieve. (*Low, to* GENE) It's the confusion and worrying about your mother.

GENE Well, everything's under control now, Dad, so let's go. We'll take a cab to my apartment, where I've got the car parked, and then I'll drive you out home.

TOM Your mother can't climb the stairs to your apartment.

GENE She won't have to. We'll just change from the cab to my car.

TOM But she might have to use the facilities.

MARGARET No. No. I'm all right.

TOM (*With a twinkle in his eye . . . the operator*) You know, if you handle it right, you can get away with parking right out there in front of the station. When I used to come to meet the Senator . . .

GENE I know, but I'd prefer to do it this way. I'm not very good at that sort of thing.

TOM Well, all right. You're the boss. It's just that you can get right on the West Side Drive.

GENE It's easier for me to go up the Major Degan.

TOM Rather than the Cross County?

GENE Yes.

TOM I don't like to question you, old man, but I'm sure if you clocked it, you'd find it shorter to go up the West Side Drive and—

MARGARET (*Annoyed with him*) Father, now come on. Gene is handling this.

TOM All right. All right. Just a suggestion.

GENE Come on, Dad.

TOM You go along with your mother. I'll keep an eye on this luggage.

GENE (*Trying to be patient*) It will be all right.

TOM (*Clenching his teeth and jutting out his jaw, sarcastic*) You don't mind if I want to keep an eye on my luggage, do you? I've traveled a good deal more than you have in my day, old man, and I know what these guys will do if you let them out of your sight. (GENE *is embarrassed. The* PORTER *smiles and starts moving off*) Hey, not so fast there.
    (*And he strides after the* PORTER *and the bags.* GENE *moves to the front of the stage again, as the lights dim on the retreating wheelchair and luggage, and on* TOM *and* MARGARET)

GENE My father's house was in a suburb of New York City, up in Westchester County. It had been a quiet town with elms and chestnut trees, lawns and old sprawling houses with a certain nondescript elegance. My father had been mayor of this town, a long time ago ... Most of the elms and chestnut trees had gone, and the only elegance left was in the pretentious names of the developments and

ugly apartment houses . . . Parkview Meadows Estates
. . . only there was no meadow, and no park, and no view
except of the neon signs of the chain stores. Some old
houses remained, like slightly frowzy dowagers. The
lawns were not well kept, and the houses were not painted
as often as they should have been, but they remained. My
father's house was one of these.

(TOM *and* MARGARET *have now started coming in
from the back*)

TOM Just look at this town.

MARGARET What, dear?

TOM (*Raises his voice in irritation*) Do you have that thing
turned on?

MARGARET Yes.

TOM I said just look at this town.

MARGARET I know, dear, but time marches on.

TOM Junky, ugly mess. When we came here . . .

MARGARET Don't get started on that. You can't play the
show over again.

TOM I can make a comment, can't I?

MARGARET But you always dwell on the gloomy side. Look
at the good things.

TOM Like what? . . . I'll bet you Murphy didn't bring the battery back for the Buick. I wrote him we'd be home today.
  (*He heads for the garage*)

MARGARET (*To* GENE) I don't know what we're going to do about that car. Your father shouldn't be driving any more. But they just keep renewing his license by mail. (*She moves stiffly, looking at her garden and trees and lawn*) I must say, there's no place like home. *Mmmmm.* Just smell the grass.

GENE (*Taking his mother's arm*) You all right?

MARGARET It's just my mean old joints getting adjusted. I want to look at my garden. I think I see some crocuses.
  (*And she moves into the shadows to see her garden*)

TOM (*Coming back*) Well, he did bring it back.

GENE Good.

TOM Can't count on anyone these days. Where's your mother?

GENE She's walking around her garden.

TOM What?

GENE She's walking around her garden.

TOM You know, Gene, I don't mean to criticize, but I notice you're mumbling a great deal. It's getting very difficult to understand you.

GENE (*Friendly, his hand on his father's shoulder*) I think you need a hearing aid, Dad.

TOM I can hear perfectly well if people would only enunciate. "Mr. Garrison, if you would only *E-NUN-CIATE.*" Professor Aurelio, night school. Didn't you ever have to take any public speaking?

GENE No, Dad.

TOM All your education. Well ... Where did you say your mother was?

GENE Walking around her garden.

TOM (*Intense. He has been waiting for someone to say this to*) I tell you, the strain has been awful.

GENE She looks well.

TOM I know. But you never know when she might get another of those damned seizures.
(*He looks at the ground and shakes his head at the problem of it all*)

GENE (*Pats his father's shoulder*) It's rough. I know.

15

TOM Well, we'll manage. She's a good soldier. But you know, she eats too fast. The doctor said she must slow down. But not your mother. Incidentally, don't forget she has a birthday coming up.

GENE (*Who knows his mother's birthday and hates being reminded of it each year*) Yes, I know.

TOM Before you go, I want to give you some money. Go get something nice for me to give her. Handkerchiefs. You know what she likes.

GENE (*Who has done this every Christmas and birthday for years . . . smiles*) All right. (TOM *coughs, deep and thick*) We're going to have to get that cough looked into.

TOM I fully intend to, now I'm home. But I wasn't going to let them get their hands on me down there. If you're a tourist, they just soak you.

GENE With the problems you've had with pneumonia . . .

TOM I can take care of myself. Don't worry about me.

GENE Let's go see if Dr. Mayberry can see you.

TOM First thing tomorrow.

GENE Why not make the appointment today?

TOM (*Irked*) Now, look, I'm perfectly able to take care of myself.

16

GENE   Mother would feel better if—

TOM   (*That smile again*)   Now, Gene, don't you think I have the sense to take care of myself?

GENE   (*Smiling, but a little angry*)   Sometimes, no.

TOM   (*Considers this, but is mollified by the smile*)   Well, I appreciate your solicitude, old man. Why don't you stay for supper?

GENE   I was planning to take you to Schrafft's.

TOM   Hooray for our side! (GENE *starts out toward the garden*) Oh, Gene. I want to talk to you a minute. We received your four letters from California . . .

GENE   I'm sorry I didn't write more often.

TOM   Well, we *do* look forward to your letters. But this girl, this woman you mentioned several times . . .

GENE   Yes?

TOM   You seemed to see a lot of her.

GENE   Yes. I did.

TOM   Carol's been dead now, what is it? . . .

GENE   About a year.

TOM   And there's no reason why you shouldn't go out with other women. (GENE *just waits*) I was in California with the Senator, and before that. It's a perfectly beautiful place. I can understand your enthusiasm for it. Gorgeous place.

GENE   Yes. I like it a lot.

TOM   But listen, Gene . . . (He *bites his upper lip, and his voice is heavy with emotion*) If you were to go out there, I mean, to live, it would kill your mother. (He *looks at his son with piercing eyes, tears starting. This has been in the nature of a plea and an order.* GENE *says nothing. He is angry at this order, that his father would say such a thing*) God, you know you're her whole life. (GENE *is further embarrassed and troubled by this statement of what he knows to be the truth from his father*) Yes, you are! Oh, she likes your sister. But you . . . are . . . her . . . life!

GENE   Dad, we've always been fond of each other, but—

TOM   Just remember what I said.
          (MARGARET *can now be heard reciting to herself, very emotionally*)

MARGARET   "Loveliest of trees, the cherry now / Is hung with bloom along the bough, / And stands about the wood-land ride, / Wearing white for Eastertide." (She *opens her eyes*) Oh, Gene, I've just been looking at your garden. Give me a real hug. You haven't given me a real hug yet.

(GENE *hugs her, uncomfortable, but loving and dutiful. It is, after all, a small thing.* MARGARET *looks at him, then kisses him on the lips*) Mmmmmmm. (*She smiles, making a playful thing of it*) Oh, you're a sight for sore eyes.
    (TOM *has watched this, and looks significantly at* GENE)

TOM (*Moving off*) Gene is staying for dinner. We're going to Schrafft's.

MARGARET Oh. Can you give us all that time?

TOM He said he would. Now come along. You shouldn't be standing so long. You've had a long trip.
    (*He exits*)

MARGARET He worries so about me. I suppose it is a strain, but he makes me nervous reminding me I should be sitting or lying down . . . Oh, well . . . (*She takes* GENE's *arm*) How are you, my precious?

GENE Fine.

MARGARET We haven't talked about your trip to California.

GENE No.

MARGARET (*Raising her voice*) I say, we haven't talked about your trip.

GENE We will.

MARGARET (*Low*)   Did you speak to your father about seeing a doctor?

GENE   He promised me tomorrow.

MARGARET   I'll believe it when I see it. He's so darned stubborn. Alice takes after him.

GENE   Oh, I got a piece of it too.

MARGARET (*Her tinkling laugh*)   You? You don't have a stubborn bone in your body.
(*We fade, as they move up and into the shadows*)

Immediately the lights come up on another part of the stage—Schrafft's.

MARY (*A pretty Irish waitress, she is just finishing setting up her table as* TOM *enters*)   Well, good evening, Mr. Garrison. Welcome back.

TOM (*The charmer*)   Greetings and salutations.

MARY   We've missed you.

TOM   It's mutual. Is this your table?

MARY   Yes.

20

TOM   Is there a draft here? I like to keep Mrs. Garrison out
of drafts.
        (*He looks around for windows.* MARGARET *and* GENE
        *come into the area. He is helping her, as she moves
        slowly and deliberately*)

MARY   Good evening, Mrs. Garrison. Nice to have you
back.

TOM   You remember Mary?

MARGARET (*Polite but reserved*)   Yes. Good evening, Mary.

MARY   You're looking well, Mrs. Garrison.

MARGARET (*As* TOM *holds the chair for her*)   But look at
him.
        (*She nods at* TOM)

MARY   We'll fatten him up.

TOM (*Smiling, flirtatiously*)   Will you do that now? Oh,
we've missed you. We've had a girl down there in Florida,
no sense of humor. Couldn't get a smile out of her.

MARY   Well, we'll have some jokes. Dry martini?

TOM (*A roguish twinkle*)   You twist my arm. Six to one.
(*He says this as though he were being quite a man to
drink his martini so dry.* GENE *finds all this by-play harm-
less, but uncomfortable*) You remember my son, Gene.

21

MARY (*Smiles*)   Yes.
   (GENE *smiles back*)

TOM   What's your pleasure, Gene . . . Dubonnet?

GENE   I'll have a martini too, please.

TOM   But not six to one.

GENE   Yes. The same.

TOM   Well!

GENE   Mother?

MARGARET   No, nothing. My joints would be stiff as a board.

TOM (*With a twinkle in his eye*)   You said you'd be stiff?

MARGARET   What?

TOM (*Raising his voice*)   You said you'd be stiff?

MARGARET   My joints. My joints.

TOM   Oh, wouldn't want you stiff. (*He thinks he's being very funny, and tries to share his laugh with* GENE, *who smiles reluctantly.* MARY *exits. To* GENE) Have I ever shown you this ring?

MARGARET   Oh, Tom, you've shown it to him a hundred times.

TOM (*Ignoring her reminder*)   I never thought I'd wear a diamond ring, but when the Senator died, I wanted something of his. Last time I had it appraised, they told me it was worth four thousand.

MARGARET   It's his favorite occupation, getting that ring appraised.

TOM (*Again ignoring her*)   Don't let anyone ever tell you it's a yellow diamond. It's a golden diamond. Of course, when I go to see a doctor, I turn it around.
      (*He gives a sly smile. The others look embarrassed*)

MARGARET (*Looking at the menu*)   What are you going to have?

TOM (*Taking out his glasses*)   Now, this is my dinner, understand?

GENE   No. I invited you.

TOM   Uh-uh. You had all the expenses of coming to get us.

GENE   No, it's mine. And order what you want. Don't go reading down the prices first.

TOM (*Smiles at the idea, though he knows he does it*)   What do you mean?

GENE Whenever I take you out to dinner, you always read down the prices first.

MARGARET Oh, he does that anyway.

TOM I do not. But I think it's ridiculous to pay, look, three seventy-five for curried shrimp.

GENE You like shrimp. Take the shrimp.

TOM If you'll let me pay for it.

GENE (*Getting annoyed*) No! Now, come on.

TOM Look, I appreciate it, Gene, but on what you make . . .

GENE I can afford it. Now let's not argue.

MARGARET Tell me, lovey, do you get paid your full salary on your sabbatical?

GENE No. Fifty percent.

TOM Well, then, look . . .

MARGARET Now, Father, he wants to pay. Let him pay. (*They consult their menus*) Incidentally, Tom, you should go over and say hello to Bert Edwards. Gene and I stopped on our way in.

TOM Why?

MARGARET   While we were gone, he lost his wife.

TOM   Where'd he lose her?

MARGARET   Tom!

TOM   Just trying to get a rise.

MARGARET   And Mrs. Bernard. She looks terrible.

TOM   Always did.

MARGARET   She lost her husband six months ago. She told me, just before we left for Florida, "I hope I go soon."

TOM   Why are you so morbid tonight?

MARGARET   I'm not morbid. They're just there. We really should see them, have them in.

TOM   Phooey! Who needs them?

MARGARET   Oh, Tom! I can't have anyone in. Your father won't play bridge or do anything. He just wants to watch Westerns or tell the story of his life.

TOM   Now, wait a minute.

MARGARET   I can't invite people to come over to watch Westerns or to listen to you go on and on. You embarrass

25

me so. You insist on going into the most gruesome details of your life.

TOM   People seem to be interested.

MARGARET   What?

TOM   Have you got that turned up?

MARGARET   Yes.
(She adjusts the volume)

TOM   I said they seem to be interested.
(He tries to take GENE *in on an exasperated shaking of the head, but* GENE *looks the other way)*

MARGARET   I admit it's a remarkable story, your life. But there are other things to talk about. People want to talk about art or music or books.

TOM   Well, let them.

MARGARET   He keeps going over and over the old times. Other people have had miserable childhoods, and they don't keep going over and over them . . . That story of your mother's funeral. And you say I'm morbid.

GENE   What was that? I don't remember that.

MARGARET   Oh, don't get him started.

TOM   Your mother wants me to play cards with a lot of women who just want to gossip and chatter about styles. That's why I won't play.

MARGARET   You won't play because you can't follow the play of the cards any more.

TOM   I beg to disagree.

GENE   Please! Don't fight . . . don't fight.
(*He's said this in a mock-serious singsong*)

MARGARET   He kept telling everyone how he wouldn't allow his father to come to his mother's funeral.

TOM (*Defensively angry*)   Are you implying that I should have let him?

MARGARET   I'm not saying—

TOM   He'd run out on us when we were kids, and I told him—

MARGARET   I'm not saying you were wrong. You're so defensive about it. I'm saying you're wrong to keep bringing it up.

TOM   You brought it up this time.

MARGARET   Well, I'm sorry. Imagine going around telling everyone he shoved his father off the funeral coach.
(*She is consulting the menu*)

TOM   And I'd do it again. I was only ten, but I'd do it again. We hadn't seen him in over a year, living, the four of us, in a miserable two-room tenement, and suddenly he shows up weeping and begging, and drunk, as usual. And I shoved him off! (*He almost relives it*) I never saw him again till some years later when he was dying in Bellevue ... of drink.
  (*The hatred and anger are held in, but barely*)

MARGARET (*She has been studying the menu*)   What looks good to you?

TOM (*A hard, sharp edge to his voice*)   I have not finished! I went down to see him, to ask him if he wanted anything. He said he wanted an orange. I sent him in a half-dozen oranges. I would have sent more, except I knew he was dying, and there was no point in just giving a lot of oranges to the nurses. The next morning he died.
  (*There is a silence for a moment, while* GENE *and* MARGARET *look at the menu, and* TOM *grips and ungrips his hand in memory of his hatred for his father*)

MARGARET (*Gently*)   Look at your menu now, Father. What are you going to eat?

TOM   I don't feel like anything. I have no appetite.
  (*He lights a cigarette*)

MARGARET (*To* GENE)   This is the way it's been.

GENE   He'll see a doctor tomorrow. Don't get upset.
  (MARY *arrives with the martinis*)

TOM   Ah, here we are.

MARY   Six to one.
    (*She puts the martini in front of him*)

TOM   Damn it.
    (*He fishes out the lemon peel*)

MARY   But you always ask for lemon peel.

TOM (*Demonstrating*)   Twisted over it, not dumped in it.
It's all right. It's all right. (*With an Irish accent*) Well,
to your smilin' Irish eyes.

MARY   He hasn't changed, has he?

TOM   What county are you from, did you say?

MARY   Armagh.

TOM   I knew there was something I liked about you. That's
where my people came from, to County Armagh. (*He
drinks*) Do you have any burnt ice cream tonight?

MARY   Ah, you.

TOM (*Smiling*)   No, I mean it. (*To* GENE) They have
burnt ice cream here.

MARY   I'll be back.
    (*And she exits.* MARGARET *sits embarrassed and*

29

piqued by this kind of flirtation which has gone on all their lives)

TOM (*The sport, to* GENE)   I like to get a rise out of them. If they kid with me, I give them a good tip. If they don't, a straight ten percent. (*He draws a line on the tablecloth to emphasize this. He looks at* MARGARET) What's the matter?

MARGARET   If you want to make a fool of yourself, go right ahead.
   (TOM *is angry, hurt and exasperated. He looks at her, and then tries to include* GENE, *to make him share his anger. But* GENE *looks away and to the menu.* TOM *stares at his glass, and his jaw muscles start to work. The scene dims in the Schrafft's area, and* GENE *moves from the table to another side of the stage)*

GENE   We hurried through the last part of our dinner. My father ate only his dessert, burnt almond ice cream. We hurried through to rush home to one of my father's rituals, the television Western. He would sit in front of them hour after hour, falling asleep in one and waking up in the middle of the next one, never knowing the difference. When my father fell in love with a program, it was forever. All during my childhood we ate our dinner to the accompaniment of Lowell Thomas and Amos and Andy. If anyone dared to talk, father would storm away from the table and have his dinner served at the radio . . . I say, we rushed away from Schrafft's. Actually, my father rushed.

We just lived down the street. I walked my mother home very slowly, stopping every fifty yards or so.

(MARGARET *has joined* GENE *and taken his arm*)

MARGARET I don't know how he can sit through hour after hour of those Westerns.

GENE I think he always wished he'd been a cowboy. "Take 'em out and shoot 'em!"

MARGARET He won't listen to the things I want to hear. Down in Florida there's only one TV in the lounge, and he rode herd on it. And then he'd fall asleep in three minutes . . . Still, he's a remarkable man.

GENE Good old Mom.

MARGARET Well, he is. Not many boys have fathers they could be as proud of.

GENE I know that, Mom. I'm very . . . proud of him.

MARGARET (*She catches his tone*) Everything he's done, he's done for his family. (GENE *just looks at her, smiling*) So he didn't dance with me at parties. (*She smiles at* GENE) You took care of that.

GENE You were just a great dancer, Mother.

MARGARET I was a terrible dancer. You just couldn't stand seeing me sitting alone at a table at the club while your father was . . .

(*She stops, realizing she's about to make* GENE's *point*)

GENE . . . off dancing with various other people, table-hopping or playing poker with the boys in the locker room.

MARGARET What a shame that children can't see their parents when they're young and courting, and in love. All they see them being is tolerant, sympathetic, forbearing and devoted. All the qualities that are so unimportant to passionate young people.
(TOM *appears*)

TOM Gene . . . Gene . . . Come watch this one. This is a real shoot-'em-up.

GENE In a minute, Dad.

MARGARET Gene, I want to talk to you.

GENE You should be in bed. You've had a big day.
(*They move to another part of the stage*)

MARGARET I took another nitro. And I've had something on my mind for a long time now. You remember you gave me that heart-shaped pillow when I was in the hospital once, when you were a boy?
(*She sits on the chaise longue*)

GENE Yes.

MARGARET   Fidget used to curl up here. (*She indicates the crook in her leg*) And you'd sit over there, and we'd listen to the Metropolitan Opera broadcasts.
(GENE *is made uncomfortable by this attempt to evoke another time, another kind of relationship, but he doesn't show it*)

GENE   Yes. I remember.

MARGARET   You'd dress up in costumes and act in front of that mirror. I remember you were marvelous as D'Artagnan in *The Three Musketeers*. (*For the fun of it, a forty-year-old-man, he assumes the dueling stance, and thrusts at his image in an imaginary mirror.* GENE *sits on a footstool and watches her adjust herself in her chaise. After a moment*) Tell me about California.

GENE   (*A little taken by surprise. Here is the subject*)   I loved it.

MARGARET   And the girl, the woman with the children? The doctor? (GENE *doesn't say anything. He frowns, wondering what to say*) You love her too, don't you?

GENE   I think so.

MARGARET   I know when Carol died, you said you'd never marry again. But I hoped you would. I know it's hard, but I think Carol would have wanted you to.

GENE   I don't know.

33

MARGARET (*Fidgets a moment from embarrassment, then*) I know it's not a mother's place to pry and talk about these things ... But I've been worried about you, I mean, you're a man ... and ... well ... sex.

GENE (*Smiles*)   I'm ... all right.

MARGARET   You mean you've been ... communicating?

GENE (*With a broad smile*)   Yes. I've been ... communicating.

MARGARET   You don't mind my talking about that, do you?

GENE (*Amused and a little embarrassed*)   No.

MARGARET   I'll never understand your generation, I guess. I'm glad I didn't have to face all ... well, all that, in my day. People simply waited. And I'm not so sure we weren't right.

GENE (*Not wanting to go into it*)   Well ...

MARGARET   Too late for me to worry about that now. Though sometimes I wish I'd known more ... understood more ... (*She stops, embarrassed.* GENE *is sad and uncomfortable that his seventy-eight-year-old mother would seem to want to talk to someone at last about her unsatisfactory sex life. The moment passes*) Gene, your sabbatical is over soon, isn't it?

GENE   A few more months.

MARGARET   I think you want to move to California and get a job teaching there and marry this woman.

GENE (*After a moment*)   Yes. I think I do. I wasn't sure while I was there. I suddenly felt I should get away and think. But when I walked into my old apartment, with all Carol's things there . . .

MARGARET   I think it would be the best thing in the world for you to get away, to marry this girl.

GENE (*Touched . . . very simply*)   Thanks.

MARGARET   A new place, a new wife, a new life. I would feel just terrible if you didn't go because of me. There are still planes, trains and telephones, and Alice comes from Chicago once or twice a year and brings the children.

GENE   Thanks, Mother. You've always made things very easy. I think you'll like Peggy.

MARGARET   I'm sure I will. You have good taste in women. And they have good taste when they like you.

GENE   I'm not so sure. I never really knew if I made Carol happy . . . If I did make her happy, I wish she'd let me know it.

MARGARET   I guess a lot of us forget to say thank you until it's too late. (*She takes his hand and smiles at him*) Thank you . . . You have such nice hands. I've always loved your hands . . . You've been so good to me, Gene, so considerate. Perhaps I've let you be too considerate. But it was your nature, and your father just withdrew behind his paper and his investments and his golf. And our interests seem to go together. You liked to sing, and I played the piano, oh, miserably, but I played. (*She strokes his hand*) I tried not to be one of those possessive mothers, Gene. If I did things wrong, I just did the best I knew how.

GENE You did everything just fine.
(*He pats his mother's hand before he draws his own away*)

MARGARET And your father has done the best he knew how.

GENE (*With no conviction*) Yes.
(*This is her old song. She knows that* GENE *knows it's probably true, but he gets no satisfaction from the knowledge*)

MARGARET Of course you know your father will object to your going away.

GENE He already has. He said it would kill you.

MARGARET How sad. Why can't he say it would kill him? He doesn't think it would hold you or mean anything to you. (*She shakes her head*) He dotes on your letters down there. Reads them and rereads them. Tells everyone what a fine relationship he has with you. "My door is always open . . . Anything he wants, he can have . . . We have always had each others' confidence . . ." (GENE *smiles at this and sadly shakes his head*) Well, you go to California. Your father and I can take care of each other. I'll remember where he put his checkbook, and he'll make the beds, which is the only thing I'm really not supposed to do. And, for your information, I have my old-lady's home all picked out. That's what I want, so I won't be a burden to any of you.

GENE   You a burden!

MARGARET   (*Wisely*) Oh, yes! Now don't mention this business to your father tonight. He's not well, and it's been such a nice day. In the next few days I'll talk to him, tell him it's important for you to—

GENE   No, I'll do it.
    (*He kisses her on the cheek*)

MARGARET   Good night, my precious.

GENE   Where would you like to celebrate your birthday?

MARGARET   Oh, lovey, you've already given me so much time. Just call me on the phone.

GENE   No . . . We can at least have dinner . . . I'll make some plans.

MARGARET   Gene, if your father gives you money to buy his present for me, please, no more handkerchiefs.

GENE   He always says handkerchiefs.

MARGARET   I know, but I've got dozens and dozens from my past birthdays and Christmases.

GENE   What would you like?

MARGARET   Get me some perfume. You choose the kind, except I don't like lily of the valley, or gardenia.

GENE   You're a hard woman to please . . . Good night . . . You look great.

MARGARET   Oh, a little rouge and lipstick. Thanks for coming to meet us. Tell your father I've gone to bed, and don't let him keep you there to all hours watching television. (*Calling after him*) I don't like carnation either.
    (GENE *waves back affectionately and moves away, as the lights dim on* MARGARET's *area.* GENE *moves, then stands and looks at the back of his father's chair as the TV sounds come up, and lights come on in that area.* GENE *moves to his father's chair and gently touches his arm while turning the knob of the TV volume*)

TOM (*Stirring*)   What? . . . What?
    (*He comes to slowly, shakes his head and looks at* GENE, *bewildered*)

38

GENE (*Gently*)   I'm going now, Dad.

TOM   Oh, so soon?

GENE (*Controls his irritation. This has always been his father's response, no matter how long he has been with him*)   Yes. I have to go.

TOM   Where's your mother?

GENE   She's upstairs. She's fine. (TOM *starts to cough*) You see about that in the morning, Dad.

TOM (*Getting up, steadying himself*)   I fully intend to. I would have done it down there, but I wasn't going to be charged outrageous prices. (*He glances at the TV screen*) Oh, this is a good one. Why don't you just stay for this show?

GENE (*The anger building*)   No, Dad. I've got to run along.

TOM   Well, all right. We see so little of you.

GENE   I'm up at least once a week, Dad.

TOM   Oh, I'm not complaining. (*But he is*) There just doesn't seem to be any time. And when you are here, your mother's doing all the talking. The way she interrupts. She just doesn't listen. And I say, "Margaret, please." . . . But she goes right on . . . Well, "all's lost, all's spent, when

39

we our desires get without content . . . 'tis better to be
that which we destroy, than by destruction dwell with
doubtful joy."

GENE (*He is always puzzled by his father's frequent use of
this quotation. It never is immediately appropriate, but it
indicates such unhappiness that it is sad and touching to
him*) We'll get a chance to talk, Dad.
(*He moves toward the porch*)

TOM   I can't tell you what a comfort it is knowing you are
just down in the city. Don't know what we'd do without
you. No hat or coat?

GENE   No.

TOM   It's still chilly. You should be careful.

GENE (*Kissing his father on the cheek*) Good night, Dad.
I'll call you tomorrow to see if you've gone to the doctor's.

TOM   Well, I may and I may not. I've looked after myself
pretty well for almost eighty years. I guess I can judge if
I need to see the doctor or not.

GENE (*Angry*) Look, Dad . . .

TOM   Seventy years ago when I was a snot-nosed kid up in
Harlem, a doctor looked at me and said if I were careful,
I'd live to be twenty. That's what I think about doctors.

Ten dollars to look at your tongue. Phooey! Out! Who needs them?

GENE Look, Dad, you're worrying Mother to death with that cough.

TOM All right, all right. I'll go. I'll be a good soldier . . . You're coming up for your mother's birthday, aren't you?

GENE Yes.

TOM And don't forget, Mother's Day is coming up.

GENE Well . .

TOM Why don't we make reservations at that restaurant in Connecticut where you took us last Mother's Day?

GENE We'll see.

TOM It will be my party. And, Gene, remember what I said about California!

GENE (*Straining to get away from all the encirclements*) Good night, Dad.
        (*He moves off*)

TOM Drive carefully. I noticed you were inclined to push it up there a little. (GENE *burns*) Make a full stop going out the driveway, then turn right.

GENE (*Angry, moves further down*) Yes, Dad.

TOM (*Calling after him*) Traffic is terrible out there now. Used to be a quiet little street. Take your first left, and your second right.

GENE (*He has driven this route for many years*) Yes.

TOM Then left under the bridge. It's a little tricky down there. (*When he gets no response, he calls*) Gene?

GENE (*In a sudden outburst*) I've driven this road for twenty years, for Christ's sake!
  (*He is immediately sorry, and turns away from his father's direction*)

TOM Just trying to be helpful.
  (*The lights fade on* TOM *as he goes back into the house.* GENE *is now downstage*)

GENE Take your first left and your second right. Then turn left under the bridge. But do not go as far as California, because it would kill your mother . . . I hated him for that, for sending up warning flares that if I left, it would not be with his blessing, but with a curse . . . as he had banished my sister Alice years ago for marrying a Jew . . . and the scene so terrified me at fourteen, I was sick . . . He knew his man . . . that part of me at least . . . a gentleman who gave way at intersections . . . And yet, when I looked at those two old people, almost totally dependent on me for

Ial Holbrook as GENE GARRISON and Lillian Gish as
MARGARET GARRISON

their happiness . . . This is the way the world ends, all
right . . .
> (*A phone rings. A light picks out* TOM *holding the
> phone*)

TOM I was downstairs in the kitchen, and suddenly I heard
your mother scream . . . "Tom! Tom!" . . . I ran up the
stairs . . . (*He is seized with a fit of coughing*) I ran up
the stairs, and there she was stretched out on the floor of
the bedroom . . . "Nitro" . . . "nitro" . . . That's all she
could say. You know we have nitroglycerine all over the
house.
> (*A* NURSE *comes to* TOM *as the lights come up; she
> leads him into a hospital waiting-room area.* GENE
> *joins them*)

GENE Dad.
> (*He shakes his hand and kisses him on the cheek*)

TOM Am I glad to see you! Have you seen your mother?

GENE Yes. She's sleeping.
> (TOM *starts to cough*)

GENE That doesn't sound any better.

TOM Well, I've had a shot. After your mother got settled
over here, the doctor took me to his office and gave me a
shot. I *would* have gone down there in Florida, you know,
but . . . well . . . (*Shakes his head*) I just don't know. I
was in the kitchen getting breakfast . . . You know I've

43

been getting the breakfasts, when suddenly I heard her scream, "Tom. Tom." I went running up the stairs, and there she was stretched out on the floor. She'd had an attack. "Nitro," she whispered. We've got it all over the house, you know. She'd had attacks before, but I knew at once that this was something more. I gave her the pills and called the doctor . . . "This is an emergency. Come quick." . . . The doctor came, gave her a shot . . . and called the ambulance . . . and here we are. (*He shakes his head, partly in sorrow, but also partly in exasperation that such a thing could happen*) She had a good time in Florida. I don't understand it. She ate too fast, you know. And the doctor had said she should do everything more slowly.

GENE There's no explaining these things, Dad.

TOM I suppose I could have seen more of her down there. But she just wanted to play bridge, and I didn't play, because the ladies just chattered all the time about styles and shops . . . And I met some very interesting people. Oh, some of them were bores and just wanted to tell you the story of their life. But there were others. You know, I met a man from Waterbury, Connecticut, used to know Helen Moffett . . . I've told you about Helen Moffett, haven't I? When I was a kid, when the clouds were low and dark, my grandfather'd take me up there sometimes on Sundays . . . a city slum kid in that lovely country . . . And Helen and I . . . oh . . . it never amounted to much. We'd go to church, and then we'd take a walk and sit in a hammock or under an apple tree. I think she liked that.

But I didn't have any money, and I couldn't go up there often. Her mother didn't like me . . . "That young man will end up the same way as his father." . . . And that scared her off . . . This man in Florida, I've got his name somewhere . . . (*He fishes out a notebook and starts to go through it*) He said Helen had never married . . . Said she'd been in love as a kid . . . and had never married. (*Tears come to his eyes*) Well, I can't find it. No matter. (GENE *doesn't know what to say. He is touched by this naked and unconscious revelation of an early and deeply meaningful love. But it seems so incongruous under the circumstances*) Some day we might drive out there and look him up . . . Helen's dead now, but it's nice country. I was a kid with nothing . . . living with my grandfather . . . Maybe if she hadn't been so far away . . . Well, that's water over the dam.

GENE (*After a long pause, he touches his father*) Yes.

TOM (*Just sits for a few moments, then seems to come back to the present, and takes out his watch*) You know, I'd like to make a suggestion.

GENE What, Dad?

TOM If we move right along, we might be able to make the Rotary Club for dinner. (GENE *frowns in bewilderment*) I've been away for three months. They don't like that very much if you're absent too often. They drop you or fine you. How about it?

(*He asks this with a cocked head and a twinkle in his eye*)

GENE   I thought we might eat something around here in the hospital.

TOM   I had lunch in the coffee shop downstairs, and it's terrible. It will only take a little longer. We won't stay for the speeches, though sometimes they're very good, very funny. We'll just say hello to the fellows and get back . . . Your mother's sleeping now. That's what they want her to do.

GENE (*Bewildered by this, but doesn't want to get into an argument*)   Let's drop by and see Mother first.

TOM   They want her to rest. We'd only disturb her.

GENE   All right.

TOM (*As they turn to go, he puts his arm around* GENE's *shoulder*)   I don't know what I'd do without you, old man.
    (*As the lights shift, and* TOM *and* GENE *head away, we move to the Rotary gathering, held in the grill room of one of the local country clubs. A piano is heard offstage, playing old-fashioned singing-type songs [badly]. A tinkle of glasses . . . a hum of men talking and laughing. This area is presumably an anteroom with two comfortable leather chairs. A man enters, wearing a large name button and carry-*

ing a glass. This is the minister, REVEREND PELL, *a straightforward, middle-aged man)*

REVEREND PELL   Hello, Tom, good to see you back.

TOM (*His face lights up in a special "greeting the fellows" type grin*)   Hello, Sam.

REVEREND PELL   Did you have a good trip?

TOM   All except for the damned wind down there. *Oooops.* Excuse my French, Sam . . . You know my son, Gene. Reverend Pell.

REVEREND PELL   Yes, of course. Hello, Gene.
            (*They shake hands*)

TOM   Gene was a Marine. (GENE *frowns*) You were a Marine, weren't you, Sam?

REVEREND PELL   No. Navy.

TOM   Well, same thing.

REVEREND PELL   Don't say that to a Marine.
            (GENE *and* REVEREND PELL *smile*)

TOM   Gene saw the flag go up on Iwo.

GENE (*Embarrassed by all this inappropriate line*)   Let's order a drink, Dad.

47

TOM Sam, I've been wanting to talk to you. Now is not the appropriate time, but some bozo has been crowding into our pew at church. You know Margaret and I sit up close because she doesn't hear very well. Well, this guy has been there in our pew. I've given him a pretty sharp look several times, but it doesn't seem to faze him. Now, I don't want to seem unreasonable, but there is a whole church for him to sit in.

REVEREND PELL Well, we'll see what we can do, Tom.

TOM (*Calling to a bartender*) A martini, George. Six to one. (*To* GENE) Dubonnet?

GENE A martini.

TOM Six to one?

GENE Yes, Only make mine vodka.

TOM Vodka? Out! Phooey!

REVEREND PELL What have you got against vodka, Tom?

TOM It's Russian, isn't it? However, I don't want to influence you. Make his vodka. Six to one, now! These fellows like to charge you extra for a six to one, and then they don't give you all the gin you've got coming to you.

REVEREND PELL I hope you don't drink many of those, Tom, six to one.

TOM   My grandmother used to give me, every morning before I went to school, when I was knee-high to a grasshopper . . . she used to give me a jigger of gin with a piece of garlic in it, to keep away colds. I wonder what the teacher thought. Phew. I must have stunk to high heaven . . . She used to put a camphor ball in my necktie too. That was for colds, too, I think . . . But they were good people. They just didn't know any better. That's my grandfather and my grandmother. I lived with them for a while when I was a little shaver, because my father . . . well, that's another story . . . but my grandfather—

REVEREND PELL   (*He puts his hand on* TOM's *arm*)   I don't mean to run out on you, Tom, but I was on my way to the little-boy's room. I'll catch up with you later.

TOM   Go ahead. We don't want an accident.

REVEREND PELL   (*As he is going, to* GENE)   You got a great dad there.
         (*And he disappears*)

TOM   I don't really know these fellows any more. (*Indicating people offstage*) All new faces. Most of them are bores. All they want to do is tell you the story of their lives. But sometimes you hear some good jokes . . . Now, here's someone I know. Hello, Marvin.
         (MARVIN SCOTT, *a man about sixty-five, enters*)

MARVIN SCOTT   Hello, Tom. Good to see you back.

TOM   You remember my son, Gene.

49

MARVIN SCOTT   Yes. Hello.

GENE   Hello, Mr. Scott.

MARVIN SCOTT (*To* TOM)   Well, young feller, you're looking great!

TOM   Am I? Well, thank you.

MARVIN SCOTT   How's Margaret?
(TOM *goes very dramatic, pauses for a moment and
bites his lip.* MARVIN *looks at* GENE)

GENE   Mother's . . .

TOM   Margaret's in an oxygen tent in the hospital.

MARVIN SCOTT (*Surprised that* TOM *is here, he looks at* GENE,
then at TOM)   I'm terribly sorry to hear that, Tom.

TOM   Heart.
(*He shakes his head and starts to get emotional*)

GENE (*Embarrassed*)   We're just going to grab a bite and
get back. Mother's sleeping, and if we were there, she'd
want to talk.

MARVIN SCOTT   I'm sorry to hear that, Tom. When did
it happen?

TOM (*Striving for control. His emotion is as much anger that
it could happen, and self-pity, as anything else*)   This

morning . . . I was in the kitchen, getting something for Margaret, when suddenly I heard her scream . . . "Tom . . . Tom . . ." and I ran upstairs . . . and there she was stretched out on the bedroom floor . . . "Nitro . . . nitro" . . . she said . . . We have nitroglycerine all over the house, you know . . . since her last two attacks . . . So, I get her the nitro and call the doctor . . . and now she's in an oxygen tent in the hospital . . .
(*The bell starts to ring to call them to dinner*)

MARVIN SCOTT   Well, I hope everything's all right, Tom.

GENE   Thank you.

TOM   What happened to those martinis? We've got to go into dinner and we haven't gotten them yet.

GENE   We can take them to the table with us.

TOM   I have to drink mine before I eat anything. It brings up the gas. Where the hell are they?
(*And he heads off*)

MARVIN SCOTT (*To* GENE)   He's quite a fella.
(*And they move off as Rotarians start singing to the tune of "Auld Lang Syne," "We're awfully glad you're here," etc.*)

As the lights fade on this group they come up on the hospital bed and MARGARET. *The* NURSE *is sitting there, reading a movie magazine. The oxygen tent has been moved away.*

51

TOM AND GENE *enter quietly, cautiously. The* NURSE *gets up.* GENE *approaches the bed.*

GENE (*Whispers to the* NURSE) Anything?

NURSE The doctor was just here. He said things looked much better.

TOM (*Too loud*) Hooray for our side.

MARGARET (*Stirs*) Hm . . . What?
(*She looks around*)

GENE Hello, Mother.

MARGARET Oh, Gene. (*She reaches as though to touch him*) Look where I ended up.

GENE The doctor says you're better tonight.

MARGARET (*Her eyes flashing*) You know how this happened, don't you? Why it happened?
(*She nods her head in the direction of* TOM, *who is at the foot of the bed chatting with the* NURSE)

GENE (*Quieting*) Now, Mother. Take it easy. He's seen the doctor. He's had his shot.

MARGARET Well!

GENE You should be sleeping.

MARGARET   That's all I've been doing. (*She takes his hand*) It makes me so mad. I was feeling so well. All the ladies down in Florida said I've never looked so well.

GENE   You've had these before, Mother. Easy does it.

MARGARET   He's seen the doctor for himself?

GENE   Yes. Just a bad cold. He's had a shot.

MARGARET   Why wouldn't he have that down there?

GENE   Mother, we'll have to go if you talk like this, because you should be resting.

TOM (*Leaving the* NURSE, *cheerful*)   Well, how goes it?

MARGARET   How do I know?

TOM (*Takes her hand and smiles*)   You look better.

MARGARET   You know I came without anything. I've still got my stockings on.

TOM (*Kidding. Very gentle*)   Well, it all happened pretty quick, my darling.

MARGARET   I'll need some things.

TOM   Your wish is our command.

GENE   I'll write it down. But don't talk too much.

53

MARGARET Toothbrush . . . some night clothes. I'm still in my slip . . . a hairbrush.

TOM We'll collect some things.

MARGARET (*Joshing*) Oh, you. You wouldn't know what to bring. Gene, you look around.

GENE Yes. Now, take it easy.

MARGARET I hate being seen this way.

TOM We think you look beautiful.

GENE Mother, we're just going to sit here now, because you're talking too much. You're being a bad girl. (MARGARET *makes a childlike face at him, puckering her lips and wrinkling her nose. She reaches out for his hand*) Those are lovely flowers Alice sent. She knows your favorites. I called her. I'll keep in touch with her. She said she'd come on, but I said I didn't think she had to.

MARGARET Did you have any dinner?

TOM We went to Rotary. Everyone asked for you.

MARGARET That's nice.
     (DR. MAYBERRY *comes into the room, in the shadows of the entrance.* GENE *spots him and goes to him*)

DR. MAYBERRY Hello, Gene. How are you?

54

GENE (*Trying to catch him before he enters the room entirely*) I'd like to—

DR. MAYBERRY (*Pleasant and hearty*) We can talk right here. She seems to be coming along very well.

GENE Good.

TOM That's wonderful news.

DR. MAYBERRY (*Kidding her*) She's tough. (MARGARET *smiles and makes a face at him*) We won't know the extent of it until we're able to take a cardiogram tomorrow. It was nothing to toss off lightly, but it looks good now.

GENE Well ... thank you. (TOM *coughs*) What about that?

DR. MAYBERRY He'll be all right. Just a deep cough. He'll get another shot tomorrow.

GENE (*Low*) You don't think we should ... stay around?

DR. MAYBERRY I wouldn't say so. And she should rest.

GENE Thanks, Doctor.
      (*They shake hands*)

DR. MAYBERRY Do I have your number in New York? I'll keep in touch with you. Your dad's a little vague about things. (GENE *jots the number on a slip of paper*) Good

55

night, Mrs. Garrison. I'm going to kick your family out now so that you can get some rest.

MARGARET (*Smiles and makes a small wave of the fingers*) Take care of Tom.

DR. MAYBERRY   He's going to be fine. (*To* TOM) Drop into the office for another shot tomorrow.

TOM (*Kidding*)   Will you ask that girl of yours to be a little more considerate next time?

DR. MAYBERRY   Oh, you can take it.

TOM   Oh, I'm a good soldier. But, wow!
    (*He indicates a sore rump*)

DR. MAYBERRY   Good night.
    (*He waves his hand and disappears*)

GENE   We'll run along now, Mother.
    (*She reaches her hand out*)

MARGARET   My precious.

GENE (*Leans down and kisses her hand*)   Good night. Sleep well.

TOM   Well, my dearest, remember what we used to say to the children. "When you wake up, may your cheeks be as red as roses and your eyes as bright as diamonds."

MARGARET (*Pouts, half-kidding*)   Just you take care of yourself. And get the laundry ready for Annie tomorrow.

TOM (*With a flourish*)   Your wish is my command.

MARGARET   I put your dirty shirts from Florida in the hamper in the guest bathroom, and my things are—

GENE (*Trying to stop her talking*)   We'll find them.

MARGARET (*To* GENE)   Thanks for coming. Don't bother to come tomorrow. Father will keep in touch with you.

GENE   We'll see. Good night.
(*He stops at the door for a little wave. She wiggles her fingers in a small motion. The lights dim on the hospital scene as* TOM *and* GENE *move away*)

TOM   Well, that's good news.

GENE   Yes.

TOM   She looks a lot better than when they brought her in here this morning, I can tell you that.

GENE   She looked pretty good.

TOM   She's a good soldier. Do you remember what she asked us to bring her? My mind is like a sieve.

GENE   I'll come along and get the bag ready and round up the laundry.

57

TOM   We should get the laundry ready tonight because Annie arrives at eight sharp, and she starts getting paid the minute she enters the door. But we could leave the bag till morning.

GENE (*Uneasy*)   I've got an early appointment at college tomorrow, Dad. I'll have to run along after we have a nightcap.

TOM   Oh, I thought you might spend the night.

GENE   I . . . uh . . . I've got an early appointment at college tomorrow.

TOM   I thought you were on your sabbatical.

GENE   I am . . . But I arranged a meeting with someone there, Dad.

TOM   You could stay and still make it.

GENE   It's very early, Dad.

TOM   We've got an alarm. Alarm clocks all over the house.

GENE   I want to change before the appointment . . . Shirt . . .

TOM   I've got plenty of shirts . . . underwear . . . socks . . .

GENE (*More uncomfortable*)   I don't wear your sizes, Dad.

TOM   I could get you up earlier, then. I don't sleep beyond five these days.

GENE *(Tense)*   No, Dad . . . I just . . . No. I'll come by and—

TOM   There may be something good on television . . . Wednesday night. I think there is . . .

GENE   . . . We'll watch a little television, Dad . . . and have some drinks . . . But then I'll have to go.

TOM *(After a moment)*   All right, old man.
    (GENE *instinctively reaches out to touch his father's arm, to soften the rejection. They look at each other a moment; then* TOM *drifts off into the dark, as* GENE *moves directly downstage)*

GENE   I sat with my father much longer than I meant to . . . Because I knew I should stay the night. But . . . I couldn't . . . We watched television. He slept on and off . . . and I went home . . . The next morning, around nine thirty, my mother died . . .
    (GENE *turns and walks upstage, as the lights dim)*

Curtain

Act Two

GENE *and* DR. MAYBERRY *enter from the rear.* GENE *is carrying a small overnight case containing his mother's things.*

GENE   Thank you for all you've done for her over the years. It's been a great comfort to her, to us all.

DR. MAYBERRY   I was very fond of her.

GENE   She was terribly worried about my father's health. Yesterday she said to me, "You know what put me here."

DR. MAYBERRY   Well, Gene, I think that's a little too harsh. She's been living on borrowed time for quite a while, you know.

GENE   Yes... Where's Dad?

DR. MAYBERRY   He's gone along to the undertaker's. He wanted to wait for you, but since we couldn't reach you this morning, he went along. We sent your mother's nurse to be with him till you arrived.

GENE   Thank you.

DR. MAYBERRY   He's all right. You know, Gene, old people live with death. He's been prepared for this for years. It may in some way be a relief. He's taken wonderful care of her.

GENE   Yes, he has.

DR. MAYBERRY   Alice will be coming on, I suppose.

GENE   I've called her.

DR. MAYBERRY   He shouldn't be staying in that house alone. (GENE *nods*) Now, you have the suitcase and the envelope with your mother's things.

GENE   Yes. I think she should have her wedding ring.

DR. MAYBERRY   Maybe you ought to check with your father . . .

GENE   No . . . Will you? . . .
(*He hands the ring to* DR. MAYBERRY *and moves away. The lights come up on the undertaker's office.* TOM *and the* NURSE *are there*)

TOM   I find that constant wind down there very annoying. Every year I think it's going to be different, but it isn't. You get a little overheated in the sun, and when you walk out from behind some shelter, it knifes into you.

GENE (*He has stood looking at his father for a moment. He now comes to him with tenderness, to share the experience*) Dad.

64

TOM (*Looks up in the middle of his story*)   Oh, Gene.
(*He gets up shakily. They embrace.* GENE *pats him on the back.* TOM *steps away and shakes his head. His mouth contorts, showing emotion and anger that this should have happened. He looks at the floor in moments like this*)

NURSE   We've given him a little sedative.

TOM (*Looks up*)   What?

NURSE   I said we'd given you a little sedative.

TOM (*At once the charmer*)   Oh, yes. This lovely lady has taken wonderful care of me.

GENE (*To the* NURSE)   Thank you.

TOM   It turns out she's been to Florida, very near to where we go.

GENE (*A little surprised at this casual conversation, but playing along*)   Oh, really?

TOM   I was telling her it was too bad we didn't have the pleasure of meeting her down there. But she goes in the summer. Isn't it terribly hot down there in the summer?

NURSE   The trade winds are always blowing.

TOM   Oh, yes, those damnable winds. We wanted this young man to come join us there, but he went to California instead. (*To* GENE) You'll have to come down to Florida sometime. See what lovely girls you'd meet there!

GENE (*Baffled and annoyed by this chatter, but passes it off*) I will.

TOM What was your name again? My mind's like a sieve.

NURSE Halsey.

TOM (*Courtly*) Miss Halsey ... My son, Gene.

GENE How do you do?

TOM Miss Halsey and I are on rather intimate terms. She ... uh ... gave me my shot.

GENE Good.

TOM (*To the* NURSE) I had this terrible cough down there. The winds. But I'll be all right. Don't worry about me. If I can get some regular exercise, get over to the club.
    (*For a moment they all just sit there. Obviously there is to be no sharing of the experience of the mother's death*)

GENE I called Alice.

TOM Oh. Thank you. (*To the* NURSE) Alice was my daughter. She ... uh ... lives in Chicago.

66

Teresa Wright as ALICE and Alan Webb as TOM GARRISON

NURSE (*Shaking his hand, kindly*) Good-by, Mr. Garrison.

TOM Oh, are you going?

NURSE Yes. Take good care of yourself.

TOM Oh, well. Thank you very much my dear. You've been very kind.

GENE Thank you.
(*The* NURSE *exits*)

MARVIN SCOTT (*Entering with some forms and papers*) Now, Tom, all we have to do is—(*He looks up from papers and sees* GENE) Oh, hello, Gene.

GENE Mr. Scott.

MARVIN SCOTT I'm terribly sorry.

GENE Thank you.

MARVIN SCOTT Now, the burial is to be where, Tom?
(*Throughout he is simple, considerate and decent*)

TOM The upper burial ground. I've got the deed at home in my file cabinet, if I can ever find it. For years I've meant to clean out that file cabinet. But I'll find it.

MARVIN SCOTT (*To* GENE) Will you see that I get it? At least the number of the plot?

GENE   It's 542.

MARVIN SCOTT   You're sure of that?

GENE   My wife was buried there last year.

TOM (*Suddenly remembering*)   That's right.
(*He reaches out and puts his hand on* GENE's *arm, implying that they have something to share.* GENE *doesn't really want to share his father's kind of emotionalism*)

MARVIN SCOTT (*He has been making notes*)   We'll need some clothes . . . uh . . .

GENE (*Quickly*)   Yes, all right. I'll take care of that.

MARVIN SCOTT   Do you want the casket open or closed while she's resting here?
(*There is a pause*)

GENE   Dad?

TOM   What was that?

GENE   Do you want the casket open or closed?

TOM   Oh . . . open, I think.
(GENE *would have preferred it closed*)

MARVIN SCOTT   Now, an obituary. Perhaps you would like to prepare something, Tom.

TOM   Yes. Well . . . Gene? Gene was very close to his mother.

(MARVIN SCOTT *looks at* GENE)

GENE   Yes, I'll work something up.

MARVIN SCOTT   If you could by this afternoon, so that it would catch the—

TOM   She was my inspiration. When I met her the clouds hung low and dark. I was going to night school, studying shorthand and typing and *elocution* . . . and working in a lumberyard in the daytime . . . wearing a cutaway coat, if you please, someone at the church had given me . . . I was making a home for my brother and sister . . . My mother had died, and my father had deserted us . . . (*He has gone hard on his father . . . and stops a moment*) "He did not know the meaning of the word 'quit.'" They said that some years ago when The Schoolboys of Old Harlem gave me an award. You were there, Gene.

GENE   Yes.

TOM   "Obstructions, yes. But go through them or over them, but never around them." Teddy Roosevelt said that. I took it down in shorthand for practice . . . Early in life I developed a will of iron . . . (*You can feel the iron in the way he says it*) Any young man in this country who has a sound mind and a sound body, who will set himself an objective, can achieve anything he wants, within

69

reason. (*He has said all this firmly, as though lecturing or giving a speech. He now looks at his cigarette*) Ugh . . . Filthy habit. Twenty years ago a doctor told me to give these things up, and I did. But when things pile up . . . Well . . . All's lost, all's spent, when we our desires get without content . . .

(*He looks around. There is a pause*)

GENE   I'll write something.

TOM   About what?

GENE   Mother. For an obituary.

TOM   Oh, yes, you do that. He's the lit'ry member of the family. You'll use the church, won't you? Not the chapel. I imagine there'll be hundreds of people there . . . Garden Club . . . Woman's Club . . . Mother's Club.

MARVIN SCOTT   I'm sure that Reverend Pell will use whichever you want. (*He shuffles some papers*) Now, Tom, the only thing that's left is the most difficult. We have to choose a coffin.

TOM   Do we have to do that now?

MARVIN SCOTT   It's easier now, Tom. To get it over with.

TOM (*Firm*)   I want the best. That's one thing. I want the best!

70

MARVIN SCOTT (*Moves across the stage with* TOM *and* GENE) There are many kinds.

TOM (*As he takes a few steps, he takes* GENE's *arm*)   I don't know what I'd do without this young fellow. (*This kind of word-bribery disturbs* GENE. *In the coffin area, overhead lights suddenly come on. Shafts of light in the darkness indicate the coffins.* TOM *claps his hand to his forehead*) Do I have to look at all these?

MARVIN SCOTT (*Gently*)   It's the only way, Tom. The best way is to just let you wander around alone and look at them. The prices are all marked on the cards inside the caskets.
     (*He lifts an imaginary card*)

TOM (*Puts on his glasses to look*)   Nine hundred? For the casket?

MARVIN SCOTT   That includes everything, Tom. All our services, and one car for the mourners. Other cars are extra.

TOM (*To* GENE, *who is standing back*)   Well, we'll have your car, so we shouldn't need another. Anybody else wants to come, let them drive their own car. (*Looks back at the caskets*) Oh, dear . . . Gene! (GENE *comes alongside. He is tender and considerate to the part of his father that is going through a difficult time, though irritated by the part that has always angered him. They walk silently among the caskets for a few moments.* TOM *lifts a price tag and looks at it*) Two thousand! (*He taps an imaginary casket*) What are these made of?

MARVIN SCOTT (*Coming forward*) They vary, Tom . . . Steel, bronze . . . wood.

TOM   What accounts for the variation in prices?

MARVIN SCOTT   Material . . . workmanship . . . The finish inside. You see, this is all silk.

TOM   I suppose the metal stands up best.

MARVIN SCOTT   Well, yes. (TOM *shakes his head, confused*) Of course the casket does not go directly into the ground. We first sink a concrete outer vault.

TOM   Oh?

MARVIN SCOTT   That prevents seepage, et cetera.

TOM   That's included in the price?

MARVIN SCOTT   Yes.
         (TOM *walks on.* GENE *stays in the shadows*)

TOM   How long do any of these stand up?
         (GENE *closes his eyes*)

MARVIN SCOTT   It's hard to say, Tom. It depends on the location. Trees, roots, and so on.

72

TOM   I suppose these metal ones are all welded at the seams?

MARVIN SCOTT   Oh, yes.

TOM   Our plot up there is on a small slope. I suppose that's not so good for wear. I didn't think of that when I bought it . . . And the trees looked so lovely . . . I never thought.

MARVIN SCOTT (*Gently*)   I don't think it makes that much difference, Tom.

TOM (*Moves along, stops*)   For a child?

MARVIN SCOTT   Yes.

TOM (*Shakes his head, moved*)   My mother would have fit in that. She was a little bit of a thing . . . Died when I was ten. (*Tears come to his eyes*) I don't remember much about her funeral except my father . . . He'd run out on us, but he came back when she died . . . and I wouldn't let him come to the cemetery. (*He gets angry all over again . . . then*) Oh, well . . . water over the dam. But this made me think of her . . . a little bit of a thing. (GENE *is touched by his father's memory of his own mother, but still upset at this supermarket type of shopping*) Five hundred. What do you think of this one, Gene? (GENE *comes up*) I like the color of the silk. Did you say that was silk or satin?

MARVIN SCOTT   Silk.

73

GENE   I don't think it makes much difference, Dad. Whatever you think.

TOM   I mean, they all go into this concrete business. (*He senses some disapproval on* GENE'*s part and moves on, then adjusts his glasses*) This one is eight hundred. I don't see the difference. Marvin, what's the difference?

MARVIN SCOTT   It's mostly finish and workmanship. They're both steel.

TOM   I don't like the browns or blacks. Gray seems less somber. Don't you agree, Gene?

GENE   Yes, I do.

TOM   Eight hundred. Is there a tax, Marvin?
       (GENE *turns away*)

MARVIN SCOTT   That includes the tax, Tom.

TOM   All right. Let's settle for that, then, and get out of here.
       (*He shivers*)

MARVIN SCOTT   Fine. (*To* GENE) And you'll send some clothes over?

GENE   Yes.
       (GENE *bobs his head up and down, annoyed with the*

74

details, though MARVIN *has been considerate and discreet*)

MARVIN SCOTT   I'd estimate that Mrs. Garrison should be . . . that is, if people want to come to pay their respects, about noon tomorrow.

GENE   All right.

MARVIN SCOTT   Would you like to see where Mrs. Garrison will be resting?

GENE (*Definite*)   No, thank you. I think we'll be moving along.

MARVIN SCOTT   I assume your sister Alice will be coming on?

GENE   She arrives this evening. (*He looks around for his father and sees him standing in front of the child's coffin, staring at it. He goes over to his father and takes him gently by the arm*) Shall we go, Dad?

TOM (*Nods his head, far away*)   She was just a little bit of a thing.
       (*And they start moving out of the room, as the lights dim out*)

As the lights come up again on another part of the stage, ALICE, GENE's *older sister, is coming on. She is in her early forties, attractive, brisk, realistic, unsentimental.*

ALICE   Shouldn't we be getting home to Dad?

GENE (*Carrying two highballs. He is blowing off steam*)
I suppose so, but I'm not ready to go home yet . . . Let's
sit over here, where we can get away from the noise at the
bar.

ALICE   You've had quite a day.

GENE   I'm sorry for blowing off, but damn it, Alice, our
mother died this morning, and I've wanted to talk about
her, but she hasn't been mentioned except as "my inspiration," which is his cue to start the story of his life.

ALICE   I'm sorry you've had to take it all alone.

GENE   Well, I'm glad as hell you're here, and I'm glad of
the chance to get out of the house to come to meet you . . .
I'm so tired of hearing about "when the clouds hung low
and dark" . . . I'm so tired of people coming up to me and
saying, "Your dad's a remarkable man." Nobody talks
about Mother. Just "He's a remarkable man." Christ,
you'd think he died! . . . I want to say to them, "My
mother was a remarkable woman . . . You don't know my
father. You only know the man in the newspapers. He's a
selfish bastard who's lived on the edge of exasperation all
his life. You don't know the bite of his sarcasm. The night
he banished my sister for marrying a Jew did not get into
the papers."

ALICE   *Shhh* . . .

GENE What a night that was! Mother running from the room sobbing. You shouting at him and storming out, and the two of us, father and son, left to finish dinner, in silence. Afterward I threw up.

ALICE I shouted and you threw up. That was pretty much the pattern.

GENE I know I'm being unfair. But I'm in the mood to be unfair. I've wanted to turn to him all day and say, "For Christ's sake, will you for once shut up about your miserable childhood and say something about Mother?" (*A little ashamed of his outburst*) But I can't say that. He's an old man and my father, and his wife has died, and he may be experiencing something, somewhere, I know nothing about. (*He shakes his head for going on like this*) I'm sorry.

ALICE It's all right.

GENE No. (*He touches her arm, smiles*) Mother loved your flowers.

ALICE I've felt guilty about Mother all the way coming here. I should have seen her more, invited her more often, brought the kids more often. Instead I sent flowers.

GENE I guess that's an inevitable feeling when a person dies. I feel the same way.

ALICE But you were so good to her. You made her life.

GENE (*He has always hated that phrase. Slowly, quietly*)
A son is not supposed to make his mother's life . . . Oh, I
loved Mother. You know that. But to be depended on to
make her life . . . Dad says, he boasts, he never knew the
meaning of the word "quit." Well, he quit on her all right.
And I . . . I was just there. (ALICE *looks at this sudden
revelation of his feelings, his resentment that he was left
to save his mother from loneliness and unhappiness*)
Still, wait till you see him. There's something that comes
through . . . the old Tiger. Something that reaches you
and makes you want to cry . . . He'll probably be asleep
when we get home, in front of the television. And you'll
see. The Old Man . . . the Father. But then he wakes up
and becomes Tom Garrison, and I'm in trouble . . . Last
night he asked me to stay with him, and I didn't . . . I
couldn't. I'm ashamed of that now.

ALICE (*Touched by the complexity of* GENE's *feelings, she
looks at him a long moment, then*) Have you called
California?

GENE (*Frowns. A problem*) No.
(*He takes a drink, wanting to avoid the subject*)

ALICE I suppose we have enough problems for the next few
days, but . . .

GENE After?

ALICE Yes. We'll have to start thinking about Dad, about
what we're going to do.

GENE (*Nods his head*)   I don't know. (*They look at each other a moment, then*) Well, let's go home. (*He rises*) Thanks for listening to all this, Alice. You had to pay good money to get someone to listen to you. I appreciate it. (*He smiles*) I thought I wanted to talk to you about Mother, but all I've done is talk about him, just like the others.

ALICE   We'll talk. There'll be time.
(*And they leave. The lights dim out on the bar area and come up on the home area.* TOM *is asleep, his head forward, his glasses on, some legal papers in his lap. Quiet like this, he is a touching picture of old age. The strong face . . . the good but gnarled hands. He is the symbol of* FATHER. *The television is on. As* GENE *and* ALICE *come in, they pause and look. They are impressed by the sad dignity. Finally* GENE *approaches and gently puts his hand on his father's arm, then turns down the television*)

GENE   Dad?

TOM (*Barely stirs*)   Hm?

GENE   Dad?

TOM   Mm? Margaret? (*Coming to a little more and looking up at* GENE) . . . Oh, Gene . . . I must have dozed off.

GENE   Alice is here.

TOM   Alice? . . . What for?
(*He is genuinely confused*)

ALICE (*Comes from the shadows*)   Hello, Dad.

TOM (*Looks around, a bit panicky, confused. Then he re-
members*)   Oh . . . Oh, yes.
   (*He bites his upper lip, and with his gnarled hands
   grips theirs for a moment of affection and family
   strength.* ALICE *kisses him on the cheek. They help
   him from the chair and start putting on his coat. As
   the lights dim on the home area, they come up on a
   graveyard area.* TOM, GENE *and* ALICE *and all the
   people we have met, are gathering as* REVEREND PELL
   starts his eulogy)

REVEREND PELL   Margaret Garrison was a loving wife and
a kind and generous mother, and a public-spirited member
of the community. The many people who were touched
by her goodness can attest to the pleasure and joy she
brought them through her love of life and her power to
communicate this love to others. The many children, now
grown . . .

GENE (*Turns from the family group*)   Only a dozen or so
people were at my mother's funeral. Most of her friends
were dead, or had moved to other cities, or just couldn't
make it. Fifteen years earlier the church would have been
filled. There were a few men sent from Rotary, a few
women from the Garden Club, the Mother's Club, the
Woman's Club, and a few of the members of her bridge
club were there . . . The hundreds of children who had
listened to her tell stories year after year on Christmas
Eve were all gone, or had forgotten . . . Perhaps some of

them who were still in the neighborhood looked up from their evening papers to say, "I see Mrs. Garrison died. She was nice ... Well, she was an old lady."
(*He turns to rejoin the family group*)

REVEREND PELL   Earth to earth ... ashes to ashes ... dust to dust ... The Lord giveth and the Lord taketh away ... Blessed be the name of the Lord ... Amen.
(TOM *comes to shake hands with* REVEREND PELL. *The others drift about, exchanging nods, and gradually leave during the following*)

TOM   Well, it's a nice place up here.

GENE (*Who has wandered over to look at another grave*) Yes.

TOM   Your mother and I bought it soon after we were married. She thought it a strange thing to do, but we bought it. (*He looks at the grave* GENE *is looking at*) Now, let's see, that's ...

GENE   Carol.

TOM   Who?

GENE   Carol. My wife.

TOM   Oh, yes. (*He reaches out a sympathetic hand toward* GENE, *then moves away*) There's room for three more burials up here, as I remember. There ... there ... and there. I'm to go there, when the time comes. (*He looks around for a moment*) This plot is in terrible shape . . . I paid three hundred dollars some years ago for perpetual care, and now look at it. Just disgraceful . . . I'm going to talk to that superintendent.

(*And he strides off. The lights change.* ALICE *and* GENE *move into another area, what might be a garden with a bench. For a moment neither says anything.* GENE *lights a cigarette and sits on the grass*)

ALICE   I don't know how you feel, but I'd like to figure out some kind of memorial for Mother . . . Use some of the money she left.

GENE   Yes, definitely.

ALICE   Maybe some shelves of books for the children's library. Christmas books with the stories she liked to tell.

GENE   That's a good idea.
(*There is a long and awkward pause*)

ALICE   Well, Gene, what are we going to do?

GENE   (*Frowns*)   Mother always said to put her in an old-people's home. She had one all picked out.

ALICE   Sidney's mother and father saw it coming and arranged to be in one of those cottage colonies for old people.

GENE   Mother and Dad didn't.

82

ALICE I think you should go ahead and get married and move to California . . . But . . . I might as well get this off my chest, it would be murder if he came to live with us. In the first place, he wouldn't do it, feeling as he does about Sid, and the kids can't stand how he tells them how to do everything.

GENE I think you're right. That would never work. (*There is a pause.* GENE *looks out at the garden*) I can't tell you what it does to me as a man . . . to see someone like that . . . a man who was distinguished, remarkable . . . just become a nuisance.

ALICE (*She is disturbed at what her brother may be thinking*) I know I sound hard, but he's had his life . . . and as long as we can be assured that he's taken care of . . . Oh, I'll feel some guilt, and you, maybe more. But my responsibility is to my husband and my children.

GENE Yes. That's *your* responsibility.

ALICE And your responsibility is to yourself . . . to get married again, to get away from memories of Carol and her whole world. Have you called California?

GENE (*Frowns*) No.

ALICE If I were the girl you were planning to marry, and you didn't call me to tell me your mother had died . . .

GENE (*Gets up, disturbed*) I just haven't wanted to go into it all with her.

83

ALICE (*Understanding, but worried*) Gene, my friend . . . my brother . . . Get out of here!

GENE Look, Alice, your situation is quite different. Mine is very complex. You fortunately see things very clearly, but it's not so easy for me. (ALICE *looks at* GENE, *troubled by what his thinking seems to be leading to. After a moment . . . reflective*) We always remember the terrible things about Dad. I've been trying to remember some of the others . . . How much he *did* do for us.

ALICE I'm doing a lot for my kids. I don't expect them to pay me back at the other end. (GENE *wanders around, thinking, scuffing the grass*) I'm sure we could find a full-time housekeeper. He can afford it.

GENE He'd never agree.

ALICE It's that or finding a home. (GENE *frowns*) Sidney's folks like where they are. Also, we might as well face it, his mind's going. Sooner or later, we'll have to think about powers of attorney, perhaps committing him to an institution.

GENE God, it's all so ugly.

ALICE (*Smiling*) Yes, my gentle Gene, a lot of life is.

GENE Now, look, don't go trying to make me out some soft-hearted . . . (*He can't find the word*) I know life is ugly.

ALICE Yes, I think you know it. You've lived through a
great deal of ugliness. But you work like a Trojan to deny
it, to make it not so. (*After a moment, not arguing*) He
kicked me out. He said he never wanted to see me again.
He broke Mother's heart over that for years. He was mean,
unloving. He beat the hell out of you when you were a
kid . . . You've hated and feared him all your adult life . . .

GENE (*Cutting in*) Still he's my father, and a man. And
what's happening to him appalls me as a man.

ALICE We have a practical problem here.

GENE It's not as simple as all that.

ALICE To me it is. I don't understand this mystical haze
you're casting over it. I'm going to talk to him tomorrow,
after the session with the lawyer, about a housekeeper.
(GENE *reacts but says nothing*) Just let me handle it. He
can visit us, and we can take turns coming to visit him.
Now, I'll do the dirty work. Only when he turns to you,
don't give in.

GENE I can't tell you how ashamed I feel . . . not to say with
open arms, "Poppa, come live with me . . . I love you,
Poppa, and I want to take care of you." . . . I need to love
him. I've always wanted to love him.
    (*He drops his arms and wanders off.* ALICE *watches
    her brother drift off into the garden as the lights go
    down in that area. The lights come up in the living
    room area.* TOM *is seated in his chair, writing.* ALICE

85

comes into the room. Small packing boxes are grouped around)

ALICE   How are you coming?

TOM   Oh, Alice, I've written out receipts for you to sign for the jewelry your mother left you. And if you'll sign for the things she left the children.

ALICE   All right.
(*Signs.* GENE *comes into the room carrying a box full of his mother's things. He exchanges a look with* ALICE, *knowing the time has come for the discussion)*

TOM   It may not be necessary, but as executor, I'll be held responsible for these things.

ALICE   Dad, I'd like to talk a little . . . with you . . . about—

TOM   Yes, all right. But first I'd like to read you this letter I've written to Harry Hall . . . He and I used to play golf out in New Jersey . . . He wrote a very nice letter to me about your mother . . . and I've written him as follows . . . It will only take a minute . . . If I can read my own shorthand . . . (*He adjusts his glasses*) "Dear Harry . . . How thoughtful of you to write me on the occasion of Margaret's death. It was quite a blow. As you know, she was my inspiration, and had been ever since that day fifty-five years ago when I met her . . . when the clouds hung low and dark for me. At that time I was supporting my younger brother and my sister and my aged grandfather in a two-room flat . . . going to work every day in a lumber mill. Providence, which has always guided me, prompted me to take a night course in shorthand and typing, and also prompted me to go to the Underwood Typewriting Company seeking a position as stenographer. They sent me, God be praised, to the office of T. J. Parks . . . and a job that started at five dollars a week, ended in 1929 when I retired, at fifty thousand a year . . ." That's as far as I've gotten at the moment.

(He looks up for approval)

GENE   Dad, I don't think financial matters are particularly appropriate in answering a letter of condolence.

TOM   Oh? *(He looks at the letter)* But it's true. You see, it follows. I'm saying she was my inspiration . . . and it seems entirely appropriate to explain that.

GENE   Well, it's your letter, Dad.

TOM *(Looks it over)*   Well . .

ALICE   Dad, I'm leaving tomorrow . . . and . . .

TOM *(Looking up)*   What?

ALICE   I'm going home tomorrow.

TOM *(Formal)*   Well, Alice, I'm grateful you came. I know it was difficult for you, leaving home. Your mother would have appreciated it. She was very fond of you, Alice.

87

ALICE   I think we ought to talk over, maybe, what your plans are.

TOM   My plans? I have many letters to answer, and a whole mess in my files and accounts. If the income tax people ever asked me to produce my books . .

GENE   They're not likely to, Dad. Your income is no longer of that size.

TOM   (*With a twinkle in his eye*)   Don't be too sure.

ALICE   I didn't mean exactly that kind of plans. I meant . . . Well, you haven't been well.

TOM   (*Belligerent*)   Who said so?

ALICE   Mother was worried to death about—
(*She stops*)

TOM   I was under a strain. Your mother's health . . . never knowing when it might happen. Trying to get her to take care of herself, to take it easy. You know, the doctor said if she didn't eat more slowly, this might happen.

ALICE   You plan to keep the house?

TOM   Oh, yes. All my things are here . . . It's a . . . It's a . . . I'll be back on my feet, and my . . . (*Points to his head*) . . . will clear up. Now this strain is over, I'm confident I'll be in shape any day now.

ALICE   I worry, leaving you in this house ... alone, Dad.

TOM   (*Looks around, very alert, defensively*)   I'm perfectly
all right. Now don't worry about me ... either of you.
Why, for the last year, since your mother's first attack,
I've been getting the breakfast, making the beds, using a
dust rag ... (*He makes quite a performance of this. It is
a gallant struggle*) And the laundress comes in once a
week and cleans up for me ... And Gene here ... if Gene
will keep an eye on me, drop in once or twice a week ...

ALICE   That's the point.

GENE   (*Low*)   Alice!

ALICE   We think you should have a full-time housekeeper,
Dad. To live here.

TOM   (*Trying to kid it off, but angry*)   Alone here with
me? That wouldn't be very proper, would it?

ALICE   (*Smiling*)   Nevertheless ...

TOM   No. Now that's final!

ALICE   Dad, Gene and I would feel a lot better about it if—

TOM   Look, you don't have to worry about me.

ALICE   Dad, you're forgetting things more and more.

TOM   Who says so?

ALICE   Mother wrote me, and—

TOM   I was under a strain. I just finished telling you.
Look, Alice, you can go, leave with a clear mind. I'm all
right. (GENE *is touched and moved by his father's effort,
his desperate effort to maintain his dignity, his standing
as a functioning man*) Of course, I will appreciate Gene's
dropping in. But I'm all right.

ALICE   We still would like to get a full-time housekeeper.

TOM   (*Bristling*)   What do you mean, you would get? I've
hired and fired thousands of people in my day. I don't
need anyone *getting* someone for me.

ALICE   Will you do it yourself, then?

TOM   No, I told you. No! (*He gets very angry. His voice
sharpens and hardens*) Since I was eight years old I've
taken care of myself. What do you two know about it?
You were given everything on a platter. At an age when
you two were swinging on that tree out there, breaking
the branches, I was selling newspapers five hours a day,
and at night dancing a jig in saloons for pennies . . . And
you're trying to tell me I can't take care of myself . . . If
I want a housekeeper, and I don't, I'll hire one . . . I've
hired and fired thousands of people in my time. When I
was vice-president of Colonial Brass at fifty thousand a
year . . . Two thousand people. And you tell me I'm in-

competent . . . to hire a housekeeper. And how many people have you hired? (*To* GENE) You teach . . . Well, all right. That's your business, if that's what you want to do. But don't talk to me about hiring and firing.

(*The children are saddened and perhaps a little cowed by this naked outburst, the defense of a man who knows that he is slipping, and an angry outburst of hatred and jealousy for his own children. Everyone is quiet for a moment . . . then*)

ALICE Dad, you might fall down.

TOM Why fall down? There's nothing wrong with my balance.

(GENE *is sick at this gradual attempt to bring to a man's consciousness the awareness that he is finished*)

ALICE Sometimes, when you get up, you're dizzy.

TOM Nonsense. (*He gets up abruptly. He makes great effort and stands for a moment, then one foot moves slightly to steady his balance . . . and the children both look away*) Now, I appreciate your concern . . . (*Very fatherly*) But I'm perfectly able to carry on by myself. As I said, with Gene's help from time to time. I imagine we could have dinner every once in a while, couldn't we, Gene . . . once a week or so? Take you up to Rotary. Some of the speakers are quite amusing.

(ALICE *looks at* GENE *to see if he is going to speak up*)

GENE Sure, Dad.

I NEVER SANG FOR MY FATHER

TOM   Give us some time together at last. Get to know each other.

ALICE *(Quietly but firmly)*   Gene wants to get married.

GENE   Alice!

TOM   What?

ALICE   Gene wants to move to California and get married.

GENE   Alice, shut up.

ALICE *(Almost in tears)*   I can't help it. You've never faced up to him. You'd let him ruin your life.

GENE *(Angry)*   I can take care of my own life.

ALICE   You can't!

TOM *(Loud)*   Children! . . . Children! *(They stop arguing and turn to their father at his command.* TOM *speaks with a note of sarcasm)* I have no desire to interfere with either of your lives. I took care of myself at eight. I can take care of myself at eighty. I have never wanted to be a burden to my children.

GENE   I'm going to hang around, Dad.

TOM   There's no need to.

92

GENE   I'll move in here at least till you're feeling better.
(ALICE *turns away, angry and despairing*)

TOM   (*Sarcastically*)   I don't want to ruin your life.

GENE   (*Angry now at his father*)   I didn't say that.

TOM   I have long gotten the impression that my only func-
tion in this family is to supply the money to—

GENE   (*Anguished*)   Dad!

TOM   —to supply the funds for your education, for your—

GENE   Dad, stop it!
(TOM *staggers a little, dizzy.* GENE *goes to his side to
steady him.* TOM *breathes heavily in and out in rage.
The rage of this man is a terrible thing to see, old as
he is. He finally gets some control of himself*)

TOM   As far as I am concerned, this conversation is ended.
Alice, we've gotten along very well for some years now
without your attention.

GENE   (*Protesting, but hating the fight*)   Dad!

ALICE   You sent me away. Don't forget that.

TOM   You chose to lead your own life. Well, we won't keep
you now.

GENE   Dad ...

TOM (*Rage again*)   I was competent to go into the city
year after year to earn money for your clothes, your food,
the roof over your head. Am I now incompetent? Is that
what you're trying to tell me?
   (*He looks at* ALICE *with a terrible look. He breathes
   heavily for a moment or two; then, shaking his head,
   he turns away from both of them and leaves, dis-
   appearing into the shadows*)

GENE (*Angry, troubled*)   For God's sake, Alice!

ALICE   I'm only trying to get a practical matter accom-
plished.

GENE   You don't have to destroy him in the process.

ALICE   I wasn't discussing his competence. Although that
will be a matter for discussion soon.

GENE   Look, Alice, just leave it now, the way it is. Don't say
any more.

ALICE   With you staying on.

GENE   Yes. You can go with a clear conscience.

ALICE   My conscience is clear.

GENE   I am doing this because I want to.

94

ALICE You're doing it because you can't help yourself.

GENE Look, when I want to be analyzed, I'll pay for it.

ALICE (*Pleading*) But I saw you. Didn't you see yourself
there, when he started to rage? Didn't you feel yourself
pull in? You shrank.

GENE I shrank at the ugliness of what was happening.

ALICE You're staying because you can't stand his wrath the
day you say, "Dad, I'm leaving." You've never been able
to stand up to his anger. He's cowed you.

GENE Look, Alice . . .

ALICE He'll call you ungrateful, and you'll believe him.
He'll lash out at you with his sarcasm, and that will kill
this lovely, necessary image you have of yourself as the
good son. Can't you see that?

GENE (*Lashing out*) What do you want us to do? Shall we
get out a white paper? Let it be known that we, Alice and
Gene, have done all that we can to make this old man
happy in his old age, without inconveniencing ourselves,
of course. And he has refused our help. So, if he falls and
hits his head and lies there until he rots, it is not our fault.
Is that it?

ALICE You insist on—

95

GENE (*Running on*) Haven't you learned on the couch that people do *not* always do what you want them to do? It is sometimes *we* who have to make the adjustments?

ALICE The difference between us is that I accept the inevitable sadness of this world without an acute sense of personal guilt. You don't. I don't think anyone expects either of us to ruin our lives for an unreasonable old man.

GENE It's not going to ruin my life.

ALICE It is.

GENE A few weeks, a month.

ALICE Forever!

GENE Alice, let's not go on discussing it. I know what I am going to do. Maybe I can't explain my reasons to you. I just know I can't do anything else. Maybe there isn't the same thing between a mother and a daughter, but the "old man" in me feels something very deep, wants to extend some kind of mercy to that old man. I never had a father. I ran away from him. He ran away from me. Maybe he's right. Maybe it is time we found each other.

ALICE Excuse me for saying so, but I find that sentimental crap! I think this is all rationalization to make tolerable a compulsion you have to stay here. You hate the compulsion, so you've dressed it up to look nice.

GENE How do you know what you're saying isn't a rationalization to cover up a callousness, a selfishness, a coldness in yourself. To make *it* smell nice?

ALICE What do you think you'll find?

GENE I don't know.

ALICE You hope to find love. Couldn't you tell from what he just said what you're going to find? Don't you understand he's got to hate you? He may not think it in his head or feel it in his heart, but you are his enemy! From the moment you were born a boy, you were a threat to this man and his enemy.

GENE That sounds like the textbooks, Alice.

ALICE He wants your balls . . . and he's had them! (GENE *stands, starts to leave the room*) I'm sorry. I want to shock you. When has he ever regarded you as a man, an equal, a male? When you were a marine. And that you did for him. Because even back there you were looking for his love. You didn't want to be a marine. "Now, Poppa, will you love me?" And he did. No, not love. But he was proud and grateful because you gave him an extension of himself he could boast about, with his phony set of values. When was he ever proud about the thing *you* do? The things *you* value? When did he ever mention your teaching or your books, except in scorn?

97

GENE   You don't seem to have felt the absence of a father.
But I feel incomplete, deprived. I just do not want to let
my father die a stranger to me.

ALICE   You're looking for something that isn't there, Gene.
You're looking for a mother's love in a father. Mothers are
soft and yielding. Fathers are hard and rough, to teach
us the way of the world, which is rough, which is mean,
which is selfish and prejudiced.

GENE   All right. That's your definition. And because of
what he did to you, you're entitled to it.

ALICE   I've always been grateful to him for what he did. He
taught me a marvelous lesson, and has made me able to
face a lot. And there has been a lot to face, and I'm grateful as hell to him. Because if I couldn't get the understanding and compassion from a father, who could I expect it
from in the world? Who in the world, if not from a
father? So I learned, and didn't expect it, and I've found
very little, and so I'm grateful to him. I'm grateful as hell
to him.
        (*The growing intensity ends in tears, and she turns
        her head*)

GENE   (*Looks in pity at the involuntary revelation of her true
        feeling. He moves to her and touches her*)   I'll stay, Alice
        . . . for a while, at least . . . for whatever reasons. Let's not
        argue any more.

ALICE   And Peggy?

GENE She'll be coming in a week or two, we'll see.

ALICE Don't lose her, Gene. Maybe I'm still fouled up on myself, but I think I've spoken near the truth about you.

GENE I keep wondering why I haven't called her, or wanted to call her. Why I seem so much closer to Carol at the moment.

ALICE (*Gently, tentatively*) The image . . . of the eternally bereaved husband . . . forgive me . . . the dutiful son . . . They're very appealing and seductive . . . But they're not living. (GENE *just stands, looking at her, thinking about what she has said.* ALICE *kisses him on the cheek*) Good night, Gene.

GENE (*His hands on her shoulders*) Good night.

ALICE (*She suddenly puts her head tight against his shoulder and holds him*) Suddenly I miss Mother so.
      (*She sobs. He just holds her and strokes her back*)

GENE Yes. (*And he holds her, comforting her, as the lights dim*)

After a few moments of darkness the lights come up on TOM *in his bedroom in pajamas and bathrobe, kneeling by his bed, praying. On his bed is a small top drawer of a bureau, filled with mementos.* GENE *comes in. He stands in the shadows and watches his father at his prayers.* GENE *does not pray any more, and he has always been touched by the sight of his father praying.* TOM *gets up and starts to untie his bathrobe.*

GENE   You ready to be tucked in?

TOM *(Smiling)*   Yes. *(Loosening his robe)* Look at the weight I've lost.

GENE *(Troubled at the emaciated body, which is pathetic. The face is ruddy and strong, the body that of an old man)* Since when?

TOM   Oh, I don't know.

GENE *(Tapping his father's stomach)*   Well, you had quite a little pot there, Dad.

TOM *(Smiling)*   Did I?

GENE   Yes.

TOM   But look, all through here, through my chest.

GENE   Well, we'll put some back on you. You've been eating pretty well this last week.

TOM *(Looking at his own chest)*   You know, I never had hair on my chest. I don't understand it. You have hair on your chest. I just didn't have any. Well, I'm confident if I could get some exercise . . . Do you remember when I used to get you up in the morning, and we'd go down and do calisthenics to the radio?

GENE (*Smiling*) Yes.

TOM (*Stands very straight, swings his arms*) One-two-three-four . . . One-two-three-four . . .

GENE Hey, take it easy.

TOM I used to swing the Indian clubs every day at lunch-time. I gave you a set once, didn't I?

GENE I think so.

TOM We'll have to dig them out. (*Starts bending exercises*) One-two-three-four . . . one-two-three-four.

GENE Why don't you wait till morning for that?

TOM Remember when we used to put on the gloves and spar down on the side porch? . . . I don't think you ever liked it very much. (*He crouches in boxing position*) The manly art of self-defense . . . Gentleman Jim Corbett . . . Now it's something else again . . . Oh, well, things to worry about. But I intend to get over to the club, play some golf, sit around and swap stories with the boys. Too bad you never took up golf. Alice could have played a good game of golf. But she had a temper. Inherited it from your mother's father. Irascible old bastard, if you'll pardon my French. (*He fishes in the bureau drawer on the bed*) I was looking through my bureau drawer . . . I don't know, just going over things . . . Did you ever see this?
(*He takes out a small revolver*)

GENE Yes.

TOM Never had occasion to use it. Oh, I took it out West one winter when we went to Arizona instead of Florida. Shot at rattlesnakes in a rock pile. (*Takes pot shots*) I don't have a permit for this any more. (*Starts putting it back in its box*) I suppose they wouldn't give me one. I don't know anyone up there any more. When I was Mayor, cops on every corner would wave . . . "Hello, Mr. Garrison . . . 'Morning, Mr. Garrison." Now, one of the young whippersnappers gave me a ticket, just before we left for Florida. Said I'd passed a full-stop sign. That's what *he* said. First ticket I had in forty or more years of driving, so keep this quiet. (*He takes out a packet of photographs wrapped in tissue paper*) Pictures . . . I think you 've seen most of them . . . The family.

GENE (*Very tentatively*) You know, Dad, I've never seen a picture of your father. (TOM *looks at him a long time. Then finally, with his hatred showing on his face, he unwraps another tissue and hands over a small picture.* GENE *looks at it a long moment*) He's just a boy.

TOM That was taken about the time he was married.

GENE I'd always thought of him as . . . the way you talked about him . . . as . . .
  (GENE *is obviously touched by the picture*)

TOM Oh, he was a fine-looking man before he started to drink. Big, square, high color. But he became my mortal enemy . . . Did I ever show you that? (*He takes out a small piece of paper*) Careful . . . When I set up a home for my brother and sister, one day we were all out, and he came around and ripped up all my sister's clothes and shoes. Drunk, of course. A few days later he came around to apologize and ask for some money, and I threw him out . . . The next day he left this note . . . "You are welcome to your burden."

GENE   And you kept it?

TOM   Yes. I never saw him again until many years later he was dying, in Bellevue, and someone got word to me, and I went down and asked him if he wanted anything. He said he'd like some fruit. So I sent him in a few oranges. He died the next day.

GENE   There must have been something there to love, to understand.

TOM   In my father? (*Shakes his head "no." Then he shows* GENE *another card*) Do you remember this? (*He reads*) "To the best dad in the world on Father's Day." That was in . . . (*Turns over and reads the notation*) 1946 . . . Yes. (*Emotional*) I appreciate that, Gene. That's a lovely tribute. I think I have all your Father's Day cards here. You know, your mother used to talk of you children as her jewels. Maybe because my interests were different, I've always said you were my dividends . . . You know, I didn't want children, coming from the background I did . . . and we didn't have Alice for a long time. But your mother finally persuaded me. She said they would be a comfort in our old age. And you are, Gene.

GENE *(Touched, but embarrassed and uncomfortable)* Well . . .

TOM *(Fishes in the drawer and brings out a sheet of paper)* A program of yours from college . . . some glee club concert . . . I've got everything but the kitchen stove in here. *(Looks over the program)* Do you still sing?

GENE *(Smiling)* Not in years.

TOM That's too bad. You had a good voice. But we can't do everything . . . I remember your mother would sit at the piano, hour after hour, and I'd be up here at my desk, and I'd hear you singing.

GENE You always asked me to sing "When I Grow Too Old to Dream."

TOM Did I? . . . I don't remember your ever singing that . . . You always seemed to be just finishing when I came into the room . . . *(Looks at GENE)* Did you used to sing that for me?

GENE *(Not a joke any more)* No . . . But you always asked me to sing it for you.

TOM Oh . . . *(Puts the program away)* Well, I enjoyed sitting up here and listening. *(He pokes around in his box and takes something out . . . in tissue paper. He unwraps a picture carefully)* And that's my mother.

GENE (*Gently*)   Yes. I've seen that, Dad. It's lovely.

TOM   She was twenty-five when that was taken. She died the next year . . . I carried it in my wallet for years . . . And then I felt I was wearing it out. So I put it away . . . Just a little bit of a thing . . . (*He starts to cry, and the deep, deep, sobs finally come and his emaciated body is wracked by them. It is a terrible, almost soundless sobbing.* GENE *comes to his father and puts his arms around him and holds him. After moments*) I didn't think it would be this way . . . I always thought I'd go first. (*He sobs again, gasping for air.* GENE *continues to hold him, inevitably moved and touched by this genuine suffering. Finally,* TOM *gets a stern grip on himself*) I'm sorry . . . (*Tries to shake it off*) It just comes over me . . . It'll pass . . . I'll get a hold of myself.

GENE   Don't try, Dad . . . Believe me, it's best.

TOM (*Angry with himself*)   No . . . It's just that . . . I'll be all right.
     (*He turns and blows his nose*)

GENE   It's rough, Dad . . . It's bound to be rough.

TOM (*Shakes his head to snap out of it*)   It'll pass . . . it'll pass . . .
     (*Starts to wrap up the picture of his mother*)

GENE   Can I help you put these things away, Dad?

TOM   No . . . No . . . I can . . . (*He seems to be looking for*

105

something he can't find) Well, if you would. (GENE *helps him wrap the pictures*) I don't know what we'd do without you . . .

> (*And together they put the things back in the box. As they do so,* GENE *is deeply moved with feelings of tenderness for his father. After a few moments he starts, with great consideration*)

GENE Dad?

TOM Yes?

GENE (*Carefully*) You remember . . . I wrote you about California . . . and Peggy?

TOM What?

GENE The girl . . . in California.

TOM (*On guard*) Oh, yes.

GENE (*Putting it carefully, and slowly*) I'm thinking very seriously, Dad . . . of going out there . . . to marry . . . and to live. (TOM *straightens up a little*) Now, I know this is your home, where you're used to . . . But I'd like you to come out there with me, Dad . . . It's lovely out there, as you said, and we could find an apartment for you, near us.

> (*This is the most loving gesture* GENE *has made to his father in his life*)

TOM (*Thinks for a moment, then looks at* GENE *with a*

smile) You know, I'd like to make a suggestion . . . Why don't you all come live here?

GENE (*Explaining calmly*) Peggy has a practice out there.

TOM A what?

GENE She's a doctor. I told you. And children with schools and friends.

TOM We have a big house here. You always liked this house. It's wonderful for children. You used to play baseball out back, and there's that basketball thing.

GENE Dad, I'd like to get away from this part of the country for a while. It's been rough here ever since Carol died. It would be good for you too, getting away.

TOM Your mother would be very happy to have the house full of children again. I won't be around long, and then it would be all yours.

GENE That's very kind of you, Dad. But I don't think that would work. Besides her work and the children, all Peggy's family is out there.

TOM Your family is here.

GENE Yes, I know.

TOM Just me, of course.

GENE   You see, the children's father is out there, and they're very fond of him and see him a lot.

TOM   Divorced?

GENE   Yes.

TOM   You know, Gene, I'm only saying this for your own good, but you went out there very soon after Carol's death, and you were exhausted from her long illness, and well, naturally, very susceptible . . . I was wondering if you've really waited long enough to know you own mind.

GENE   I know my own mind.

TOM   I mean, taking on another man's children. You know, children are far from the blessing they're supposed to be . . . And then there's the whole matter of discipline, of keeping them in line. You may rule them with a rod of iron, but if this father—

GENE (*Cutting in*)   I happen to love Peggy.

TOM (*Looks at* GENE *a long moment*)   Did you mention this business of California to your mother?

GENE (*Gets the point, but keeps level*)   She mentioned it to me, and told me to go ahead, with her blessings.

TOM   She would say that, of course . . . But I warned you.

GENE (*Turns away*)   For God's sake—

TOM (*Giving up, angry*)   All right, go ahead. I can manage ... (*His sarcasm*) Send me a Christmas card ... if you remember.

GENE (*Enraged*)   Dad!

TOM   What?

GENE   I've asked you to come with me!

TOM   And I've told you I'm not going.

GENE   I understand that, but not this "send me a Christmas card, if you remember."

TOM   I'm very sorry if I offended you. Your mother always said I mustn't raise my voice to you. (*Suddenly hard and vicious*) Did you want me to make it easy for you the way your mother did? Well, I won't. If you want to go, go!

GENE   God damn it ...

TOM (*Running on*)   I've always known it would come to this when your mother was gone. I was tolerated around this house because I paid the bills and—

GENE   Shut up!

TOM (*Coming at him*)   Don't you—

GENE (*Shouting*)   Shut up! I asked you to come with me.

What do you want? What the hell do you want? If I lived here the rest of my life, it wouldn't be enough for you. I've tried, God damn it, I've tried to be the dutiful son, to maintain the image of the good son . . . Commanded into your presence on every conceivable occasion . . . Easter, Christmas, birthdays, Thanksgiving . . . Even that Thanksgiving when Carol was dying, and I was staying with her in the hospital. "We miss you so. Our day is nothing without you. Couldn't you come up for an hour or two after you leave Carol?" You had no regard for what was really going on . . . My wife was dying!

TOM   Is it so terrible to want to see your own son?

GENE   It is terrible to want to possess him . . . entirely and completely!

TOM (*Coldly . . . after a moment*)   There will be some papers to sign for your mother's estate. Be sure you leave an address with my lawyer . . .

GENE (*Cutting in*)   Dad!

TOM (*Cutting, with no self-pity*)   From tonight on, you can consider me dead. (*Turns on him in a rage of resentment*) I gave you everything. Since I was a snot-nosed kid I've worked my fingers to the bone. You've had everything and I had nothing. I put a roof over your head, clothes on your back—

GENE   Food on the table.

TOM —things I never had.

GENE I know!

TOM You ungrateful bastard!

GENE (*Seizes him, almost as though he would hit him*) What do you want for gratitude? Nothing, nothing would be enough. You have resented everything you ever gave me. The orphan boy in you has resented everything. I'm sorry as hell about your miserable childhood. When I was a kid, and you told me those stories, I used to go up to my room at night and cry. But there is nothing I can do about it . . . and it does not excuse everything . . . I *am* grateful to you. I also admire you and respect you, and stand in awe of what you have done with your life. I will never be able to touch it. (TOM *looks at him with contempt*) But it does not make me love you. And I wanted to love you. (TOM *snorts his disbelief*) You hated your father. I saw what it did to you. I did not want to hate you.

TOM I don't care what you feel about me.

GENE I do! (*He moves away from his father*) I came so close to loving you tonight . . . I'd never felt so open to you. You don't know what it cost me to ask you to come with me . . . when I have never been able to sit in a room alone with you . . . Did you really think your door was always open to me?

TOM It was not my fault if you never came in.

GENE (*Starts to move out*) Good-by, Dad. I'll arrange for someone to come in.

TOM (*Shouting*) I don't want anyone to come in! I can take care of myself! I have always had to take care of myself. Who needs you? Out! . . . I have lived each day of my life so that I could look any man in the eye and tell him to *go to hell!*
(*This last, wildly at* GENE. *The lights dim out quickly, except for a lingering light on* GENE)

GENE (*After a few moments*) That night I left my father's house forever . . . I took the first right and the second left . . . and this time I went as far as California . . . Peggy and I visited him once or twice . . . and then he came to California to visit us, and had a fever and swollen ankles, and we put him in a hospital, and he never left . . . The reason we gave, and which he could accept, for not leaving . . . the swollen ankles. But the real reason . . . the arteries were hardening, and he gradually over several years slipped into complete and speechless senility . . . with all his life centered in his burning eyes. (*A* NURSE *wheels in* TOM, *dressed in a heavy, warm bathrobe, and wearing a white linen golf cap to protect his head from drafts. The* NURSE *withdraws into the shadows*) When I would visit him, and we would sit and look at each other, his eyes would mist over and his nostrils would pinch with emotion . . . But I never could learn what the emotion was . . . anger . . . or love . . . or regret . . . One day, sitting in his wheelchair and staring without comprehension at television . . . he died . . . alone . . .

without even an orange in his hand. (*The light fades on* TOM) Death ends a life . . . but it does not end a relationship, which struggles on in the survivor's mind . . . toward some resolution, which it never finds. Alice said I would not accept the sadness of the world . . . What did it matter if I never loved him, or if he never loved me? . . . Perhaps she was right . . . But, still, when I hear the word "father" . . . (*He cannot express it . . . there is still the longing, the emotion. He looks around . . . out . . . as though he would finally be able to express it, but he can only say . . .*) It matters.

(*He turns and walks slowly away, into the shadows . . . as the lights dim*)

Curtain

About the Author

ROBERT ANDERSON was born in New York City in 1917, attended Phillips Exeter Academy and was graduated from Harvard University in 1939. During the following three years, earning his M.A. at Harvard and completing courses toward a Ph.D., he wrote twenty-one one-act plays, wrote the book, music and lyrics for college musicals, did drama criticism, and taught drama and writing courses. He then served for four years as a naval officer in the Pacific during World War II; during that time he wrote *Come Marching Home*, which won the National Theatre Conference prize for the best play written by a serviceman on overseas duty.

In 1953 Mr. Anderson's first Broadway play, *Tea and Sympathy*, opened, and became the longest-running hit in the twenty-one-year history of The Playwrights' Company. On the night before *Tea and Sympathy* opened in New Haven, Mr. Anderson became a member of The Playwrights' Company, which also produced his *All Summer Long* in 1954 and *Silent Night, Lonely Night* in 1959. Prior to the production of *Tea and Sympathy*, he wrote extensively for television and radio, and started the playwriting courses at the Actors Studio and the American Wing Theatre, where he taught for four years. He was one of the original members of The New Dramatists, and was president of the group for one year. When *I Never Sang for My Father* opened in New York in January, 1968, Mr. Anderson's hit comedy *You Know I Can't Hear You When the Water's Running* was approaching its first year as a Broadway success. Mr. Anderson has written screenplays, notably *The Nun's Story* and *The Sand Pebbles*. He is married to Teresa Wright, the actress, and they live in Connecticut.